Preface

For many students, the paper assigned in their first-year history survey is also their introduction to writing a college-level essay. Though many students understand that college papers must do more than restate information gleaned from lectures and books, they may have only a vague idea of how to go about researching, writing, and documenting a history paper. Instructors, for their part, must convey a great deal of information about history and historical methodology in a limited amount of time, often in large lecture classes; thus, they can devote only very limited time to writing instruction. *A Pocket Guide to Writing in History* is designed to aid the instructor and provide guidance for the student in just such situations.

Like the three earlier versions, this new edition of *A Pocket Guide to Writing in History* is brief and can be tucked into a pocket or backpack. It maintains the most valuable features of earlier versions — introducing students to conventions of writing in history and to researching, quoting, paraphrasing, and documenting sources, providing an overview of typical assignments, and offering extensive coverage of the computer as a research and writing tool. In addition, it includes over sixty documentation models based on the *Chicago Manual of Style* along with excerpts from a student paper. This fourth edition has been reorganized to make it even more accessible for students.

- A new chapter on working with historical sources consolidates guidance on identifying and evaluating primary, secondary, and Internet sources and helps students gain essential critical skills.
- A new chapter on understanding and avoiding plagiarism expands and consolidates coverage, raising student consciousness about what constitutes plagiarism and helping students determine both how to paraphrase and cite print sources and how to download Internet sources carefully.
- Expanded coverage of thesis statements focuses on developing a working thesis. New examples of ineffective and effective thesis statements, introductory

and closing paragraphs, and transitions between paragraphs clearly distinguish between unsatisfactory and strong student work.

- The appendices highlight the most recent and helpful indexes, references, periodicals, and Internet sources as places for students to start their research.
- The resources listed in Appendix B have been reorganized geographically, with more examples drawn from American history, for greater accessibility.

While preparing this manuscript I benefitted from the advice and encouragement of my colleagues and students at Trinity College in Washington, D.C. I am especially indebted to nineteen student reviewers and to the following historians for their thoughtful reviews of the third edition: David Berry, Rich Mountain Community College; Alice-Catherine Carls, University of Texas at Martin; Robert Fairbanks, University of Texas at Arlington; Michael Gabriel, Kutztown University; Eric Hanne, Florida Atlantic University at Boca Raton; Caroline Litzenberger, Portland State University; Harold Marcuse, University of California at Santa Barbara; Kathleen Parrow, Black Hills State University; and Christopher Snyder, Marymount University. Their suggestions and advice have been invaluable in the production of this text.

At Bedford/St. Martin's, I would like to thank Chuck Christensen and Joan Feinberg, who conceived the idea for this book. I would also like to thank my patient and insightful developmental editor, Rachel L. Safer, who has seen this edition through from its beginning; Patricia A. Rossi, Publisher for History; my production editor, Kendra LeFleur; and copyeditor, Lisa Wehrle.

I would also like to thank Susan Craig, director of the Sr. Helen Sheehan Library at Trinity College, who updated the detailed list of research sources that forms Appendix B of this manual. Finally, special thanks to Martin, Geoffrey, and Jonathan Chandler, whose love and support make my work possible.

Mary Lynn Rampolla
Trinity College
Washington, D.C.

1

Introduction: *Why Study History?*

On the original television police series *Dragnet,* Sergeant Joe Friday curbed the speculations of his witnesses with a stern admonition: "Just the facts, Ma'am. Just the facts." Students who take their first college history class with a sense of foreboding often think that historians, like Joe Friday, are interested only in compiling lists of names, dates, places, and "important" events that happened sometime in the past. But history is much more than this. The historian's goal is to acquire insight into the ideas and realities that shaped the lives of men and women of earlier societies. Some of the beliefs and institutions of the past may seem alien to us; others are all too familiar. But in either case, when we study the people of the past, what we are really learning about is the rich diversity of human experience. The study of history is the study of the beliefs and desires, practices and institutions, of human beings.

Contrary to popular belief, history does *not* repeat itself. So why should people bother studying the past in our increasingly future-oriented society? There are as many answers to this question as there are historians. First of all, a thoughtful examination of the past can tell us a great deal about how we came to be who we are. When we study history, we are looking at the roots of modern institutions, ideas, values, and problems. Second, the effort we put into grappling with the assumptions and world views of earlier societies teaches us to see the world through different eyes. The ability to perceive and recognize the meaning of events from a perspective other than our own and to appreciate the diversity of human beliefs and cultures is of inestimable value in our increasingly complex and multicultural society. Moreover, an awareness of various perspectives encourages students of history to engage in a critical analysis of their own culture and society and to recognize and critique their own assumptions. Finally, while historians don't have crystal balls with which to predict the future, an understanding of the ways the events of the past have shaped the complex problems with which we are grappling in our own times can provide us with the kind of insight that will help us make the decisions that will shape our future.

History is a complex discipline, and historians are a diverse group. They take different approaches to their material; they interpret the events of the past in different ways; they even disagree on such basic issues as whether and to what extent historians can be objective. Regardless of their approaches, however, historians see writing as an important tool of inquiry and communication.

In addition to introducing you to some of the basic elements of what historians do, this manual provides guidelines for writing papers in the field of history. Of course, the vast majority of students enrolled in their first history course are not contemplating a career in history. Indeed, most history majors follow career paths that lead them away from the study of the past into fields like law, government, business, and international relations. Nevertheless, the techniques you will need to master to write an effective history paper — how to read critically, think analytically, argue persuasively, and write clearly — are skills that will be useful to you wherever your academic interests take you and that you will value in whatever career path you choose to follow.

1a. Historical questions

Historians come to their work with a deep curiosity about the past; to satisfy that curiosity, they ask questions. It has been suggested that historians are like detectives; it is certainly true that they ask some of the same questions: *Who? What? When? Where?* and *Why?* Some of these questions are designed to elicit "the facts" and are relatively easy to answer: *Who* was the emperor of Japan during World War II? *What* tools did eighteenth-century weavers use? *When* did the Vietnamese drive the Khmer Rouge out of Phnom Penh? *Where* did the first Continental Congress meet? Other questions, however, are less easy to answer: *Who* was Jack the Ripper? *What* were the religious beliefs of the peasants of twelfth-century Languedoc? *When* did President Nixon learn about the Watergate break-in? *Where* did the inhabitants of the original settlement at Roanoke go, and *why* did they disappear? More complex questions such as these have formed the basis of absorbing historical studies.

Historians also ask questions that help them analyze relationships between historical facts. Many of the questions historians ask, for example, reflect their interest in understanding the **context** in which the events of the past occurred. For example, a historian interested in nineteenth-century science would not simply describe great "advances," such as Charles Darwin's articulation of the theory of evolution by means of natural selection. Rather, the historian would also ask questions about historical context: What role did political issues play in the acceptance or rejection of Darwin's theory? What other theories were current at the time, and how did they influence Darwin's thinking? Why did some theologians find his ideas threatening to religion, while others did not? What impact did larger social, political, and intellectual movements and institutions have on the study of biology in this period? In other words, historians do not examine events in isolation; rather, they try to understand the people and events of the past in terms of the unique historical context that helped to shape them.

As they explore the relationships between and among events in the past, historians also ask about the **causes** of events. The historical events that you will be studying and writing about can almost never be traced to a single cause, and historians are careful to avoid simplistic cause-and-effect relationships as explanations for events. For example, although the assassination of Archduke Franz Ferdinand was the event that precipitated World War I, no historian would argue that it *caused* the war. Rather, historians try to uncover the complex multiplicity of causes that grow out of the historical context in which events occurred.

Historians also ask questions about the relationship between **continuity** (events, conditions, ideas, and so on that remain the same over time) and **change.** Many of the questions historians ask reflect this interest. For example, a historian who asks "What impact did the Black Death have on the economic and legal status of the peasants?" is interested in examining the changes brought about by the bubonic plague against the backdrop of the ongoing institution of serfdom.

Finally, while the past doesn't change, historians' interests — and the questions they ask — do. Historians, like the people they study, are part of a larger context.

They are guided in their choice of subject and in their questions by their own interests and by the interests and concerns of their societies. As they ask new questions, historians look at sources in new ways. They may even discover "new" sources — sources that had always existed but had been ignored or dismissed as irrelevant. History, therefore, is a vital and dynamic discipline. We will never know all there is to know about the past because we are constantly posing new questions, and our questions, in turn, help us to see the past in new ways.

The best way to enter the world of the historian is to ask as many questions as you can about the particular historical issues you are studying. As you seek the answers to your questions, be aware of the new and more complex questions that your answers raise, and let them guide your exploration further.

1b. How this manual can help you

When you do research and writing in a history course, you become a participant in historical debate. You devise questions about historical topics, seek answers to those questions in historical sources, and come to conclusions about those topics. In the papers you write, you need to construct arguments about the conclusions you have reached and offer support for them. This manual will help you understand the process from start to finish.

Chapter 2 introduces you to working with historical sources. Chapter 3 walks you through some typical assignments given in history courses, while Chapter 4 is devoted entirely to the research paper. In Chapter 5, you will find information about the conventions of writing that guide historians. Chapters 6 and 7 are designed to help you use sources effectively while avoiding plagiarism. In addition, Chapter 7 includes models for documenting the sources you are most likely to use in an undergraduate history paper. Finally, Appendix A lists additional guides to writing in history, while Appendix B provides a guide to resources students might wish to consult while doing research.

History, like the other arts and sciences, provides a window onto the ideas and beliefs, the actions and passions, of human beings. Reading and writing history entail above all an exploration of who and what we are. This manual is designed to aid you in such exploration and to help you discover the pleasures of studying history.

2
Working with Sources

As you begin to think about historical questions, you will find that your search for answers will require you to explore a wide variety of sources. You will examine written materials of all sorts. You will look at materials written in the period you are studying and read books and articles written by modern historians. You may examine maps and photographs, paintings, and pottery. Ultimately, you may discover that you need to broaden your knowledge in a wide variety of areas, for history often takes its practitioners into all manner of related fields: literary criticism, art history, and archaeology; political science, economics, and sociology. But in any case, you will need to learn how to work with the sources on which the study of history is based.

2a. Identifying historical sources

To answer their questions, historians evaluate, organize, and interpret a wide variety of sources. These sources fall into two broad categories: *primary sources* and *secondary sources*. To study history and write history papers, you will need to know how to work with both kinds of sources.

2a-1. Primary sources

Primary sources are materials produced by people or groups directly involved in the event or topic under consideration, either as participants or as witnesses. Examples of primary sources include eyewitness accounts, letters, diaries, newspaper and magazine articles, speeches, autobiographies, treatises, census data, and marriage, birth, and death registers. In addition, historians sometimes examine primary sources that are not written — like coins, works of art, films, recordings, and archaeological remains. For recent history, oral sources, such as interviews with World War II veterans or Holocaust survivors, can also be primary sources. By examining primary sources, historians gain insights into the thoughts, behaviors, and experiences of the people of the past.

When using a written primary source, it is important to *read the source itself*. Do not simply rely on another historian's analysis of the source. The purpose of writing history, after all, is to develop your *own* interpretation based on the evidence you have assembled. If possible, you should read the whole source rather than excerpts; when you are writing a history paper, you need to know the *significance* of the entire document and the context of any portions of the source that you wish to discuss or quote. Moreover, in the process of choosing excerpts, an editor is making a judgment about what aspects of the source are important. In effect, he or she is determining the significance of the source for you. However, sources can yield different kinds of information depending on the questions the historian asks; therefore, it is preferable to read primary sources in their entirety.

2a-2. Secondary sources

Historians also use *secondary sources*: books and articles in scholarly journals that comment on and interpret primary sources. Secondary sources are extremely useful. Reading secondary sources is often the simplest and quickest way to become informed about what is already known about the subject you are studying. In addition, reading scholarly books and articles will inform you about the ways in which other historians have understood and interpreted events. Finally, secondary sources can be an important research tool. Reading them carefully can help you find a subject for a research paper by pointing you toward topics that have not yet been explored fully or about which there is controversy. Moreover, the bibliographies of secondary sources can direct you to primary sources. As valuable as they are, however, you should never base a history paper entirely on secondary sources. Whenever possible, you should study the events of the past in the words of people who experienced, witnessed, or participated in them.

2a-3. Primary or secondary?

The status of a source as primary or secondary depends on the question you ask. If you are writing about the reign of the English king Richard III (1483–85), your primary sources might include edicts, chronicles composed by contemporary witnesses to the events of his reign, and letters written by foreign ambassadors to the English court. Strictly speaking, Sir Thomas More's *History of Richard III,* written in the early sixteenth century, would be a secondary source because More was not a witness to the events he describes, and he records only the evidence provided to him by others. If, however, you are writing about the depiction of Richard III in the early Tudor period, More would be a primary source.

2a-4. Analyzing and interpreting sources

If sources always told the truth, the historian's job would be much easier — and also rather boring. But sources, like witnesses in a murder case, often lie. Sometimes they lie on purpose, telling untruths to further a specific ideological, philosophical, or political agenda. Sometimes they lie by omission, leaving out bits of information that are crucial to interpreting an event. Sometimes sources mislead unintentionally because the author was not aware of all the facts, misinterpreted the facts, or was misinformed. Many are biased, either consciously or unconsciously, and contain unstated assumptions; all reflect the interests and concerns of their authors. In any case, historians' sources often conflict; two different sources may tell two very different stories. As a result, one of the challenges historians face in writing a history paper is evaluating the reliability and usefulness of their sources.

One way in which historians evaluate primary sources is to compare them; a fact or description contained in one source is more likely to be accepted as trustworthy if other sources support or corroborate it. Another technique historians use to evaluate the reliability of a source is to identify the author's biases. We might be less inclined, for example, to believe Polydore Vergil's assertion that Richard III killed his nephews if we realize that he was the official court historian for Henry VII, who killed Richard in battle and seized the English throne for himself. Historians also read their sources carefully for evidence of internal contradictions or logical inconsistencies, and they pay attention to their sources' use of language, since the adjectives and metaphors an author uses can point to hidden biases and unspoken assumptions.

Secondary sources may also contradict each other. Several historians can examine the same set of materials and interpret them in very different ways. Similarly, historians can try to answer the same questions by looking at different kinds of evidence or by using different methods to gather, evaluate, and interpret evidence. You can use the same techniques to evaluate a secondary source as you would use to evaluate a primary source. Compare each source with other secondary sources, identify biases and unconscious assumptions, and look for logical inconsistencies. Most important, however, you should return wherever possible to the primary sources and consider whether the author uses and interprets the sources appropriately. The study of the ways in which historians have interpreted the past is called *historiography,* and knowing how to read and evaluate the work of other historians is so important that some professors may ask you to write a historiographic essay (see 3b-6). In any case, to get the most out of your reading of secondary sources, you will need to study a variety of interpretations of historical events and issues and learn how to read carefully and critically.

2b. Evaluating sources

The questions that historians pose of their sources depend in part on the nature of the sources they are working with.

Both primary and secondary sources can provide valuable information; however, they provide different kinds of information. In studying nineteenth-century communes, for example, primary sources such as the diaries or letters of commune members can provide firsthand information about the thoughts, feelings, and daily lives of the people who lived in them. Primary sources would be less useful, however, in establishing the larger, sociological effects of communal living. To get a better understanding of those effects, secondary sources in which historians offer a broader perspective on communes, perhaps examining several such communities over time, might prove more useful. (See 2a for a fuller discussion of primary and secondary sources.)

2b-1. Evaluating primary sources

Primary sources form the basic material of the historian. Nevertheless, historians do not take the evidence provided by such sources simply at face value. Like good detectives, they evaluate the evidence, approaching their sources analytically and critically.

Since primary sources originate in the actual period under discussion, we might be inclined to trust what they say implicitly. After all, if the author is an eyewitness, why should anyone doubt his or her word? However, as any police investigator could tell you, eyewitnesses see different things and remember them in different ways. The previous section noted some issues that historians take into consideration in evaluating primary sources (see 2a). In general, when you deal with primary sources, you should always ask the following:

- Who is the author?
- How does the author's gender and socioeconomic class compare to the people about whom he or she is writing?
- Why did he or she write the source?
- Who was the intended audience?
- What unspoken assumptions does the text contain?
- Are there detectable biases in the source?
- When was the source composed?
- What is the historical context in which the source was written and read?
- Are there other contemporary sources to compare against this one?

EVALUATING PRIMARY SOURCES: AN EXAMPLE. In a letter written to Sheik El-Messiri in 1798, Napoleon expresses the hope that the sheik will soon establish a government in Egypt based on the principles of the Qu'ran, the sacred text of Islam. Those principles, according to Napoleon, "alone are true and capable of bringing happiness to men."[1] Should we assume, on the evidence of this letter, that Napoleon believed in the truth of Islam? A historian might ask, "Do we have any other evidence for Napoleon's attitude toward Islam?" "What do other primary sources tell us about Napoleon's attitude toward religions such as Catholicism, Protestantism, and Judaism?" "Do any other primary sources contradict the attitude toward Islam expressed in Napoleon's letter to the sheik?" In other

1. Napoleon Bonaparte, "Letter to the Sheik El-Messiri," in *The Mind of Napoleon: A Selection from His Written and Spoken Words,* 4th ed., trans. and ed. J. Christopher Herold (New York: Columbia University Press, 1969), 104.

words, "How accurately and to what extent can this source answer questions about Napoleon's religious beliefs?" In addition, historians try to understand or interpret their sources even if those sources do not offer the best or most accurate information on a certain topic. As it happens, Napoleon did not believe in Islam. This does not mean, however, that his letter to the sheik should be relegated to the dustbin. Instead, a good historian will ask, "Under what circumstances did Napoleon write this letter?" "Who was Sheik El-Messiri, and what was his relationship to Napoleon?" "What does this letter tell us about Napoleon's willingness to use religion to his political advantage?" Thus, to write about historical questions, you will need to know how to approach many different kinds of primary sources and ask appropriate questions of them.

THINKING ABOUT EDITIONS AND TRANSLATIONS. When professional historians work with primary sources, they travel to archives and libraries around the world to work directly with the original letters, manuscripts, photographs, and so on that make up their primary sources. When they turn to published editions of their sources, they work with these sources in their original languages. Undergraduates rarely have the opportunity or the linguistic skills to conduct this kind of research. Instead, students rely on published editions of primary sources in translation or, increasingly, on documents posted on the Internet, which is an excellent source for a wide variety of documents, photographs, and other primary materials.

Using modern editions of sources in translation is an excellent way to enter into the world view of the people you are studying. Nevertheless, you should be aware that any edited text reflects, to some extent, the interests and experiences of the editor or translator. For example, when Elizabeth Agassiz compiled the letters of her husband, the nineteenth-century naturalist Louis Agassiz, for publication, she eliminated passages that reveal the strong antipathy he felt toward blacks. It was only when he examined the original letters themselves that Harvard University professor Stephen Jay Gould discovered that the published letters had been expurgated.[2] Similarly, as noted earlier (2a-1), the process by which the editor of a document collection selects which documents to include

2. Stephen Jay Gould, *The Mismeasure of Man* (New York: W. W. Norton and Co., 1981), 77.

and which to leave out also involves *interpretation.* The collection, as it appears in print, reflects how the editor interprets and organizes the material and what he or she sees as significant. The following suggestions will help you use both print and online sources most effectively:

- Always read the preface and introduction carefully to determine the principles underlying the editor's process of selection.
- Pay careful attention to the footnotes and endnotes, which will alert you to alternate readings or translations of the material in the text.
- When using an online source, follow the links that lead you to further sources or information.
- As a rule, use the most recent edition, which reflects the current state of scholarship.

NOTE FOR INTERNET USERS. The Internet is an excellent source for many primary materials. Nevertheless, it is important to remember that to abide by copyright laws, some Web sites, particularly those dealing with older materials, may post translations of sources that are in the "public domain." (A reputable Web site will inform you if this is the case.) Translations that are in the public domain were made so long ago that they are no longer covered by copyright restrictions. In such a case, the Internet is still an extremely useful tool for making you aware of the wide variety of sources that are available, but once you find a source you intend to use, you will probably want to look elsewhere for the most recent printed edition or translation.

2b-2. Evaluating secondary sources

Reading secondary sources helps us understand how other historians have interpreted the primary sources for the period being studied. Students sometimes hesitate to question the conclusions of established scholars; nevertheless, as with primary sources, it is important to read secondary sources critically and analytically, asking the same questions you ask of primary sources. In addition, the following questions are especially important to think about when you use a secondary source:

WHEN WAS THE SOURCE PUBLISHED? If it is important that you know the most recent theories about a historical subject, you should pay special attention to the publication dates of the sources you are considering. A 2000 article reviewing theories about the construction of Native American burial mounds may contain more recent ideas than a 1964 review. You should not assume, however, that newer interpretations are always better; some older works have contributed significantly to the field and may offer interpretations that are still influential. (As you become more experienced in historical research, you will be able to determine which older sources are still useful.) Moreover, older sources might offer a historical perspective on how interpretations of an issue or event have changed over time.

DOES THE AUTHOR PROVIDE SUFFICIENT AND LOGICAL SUPPORT FOR HIS OR HER THESIS? Any book or article makes an argument in support of a thesis. (For detailed information on what a thesis is and a discussion of how the thesis relates to the argument of a paper, see 5a-2). Once you have identified the thesis, you should evaluate the evidence the author uses to support it. You may not be in a position to judge the accuracy of the evidence, although you will build expertise as you continue to read about the subject. You can, however, evaluate the way in which the author uses the evidence he or she presents. You might ask yourself whether the evidence logically supports the author's point. For example, Margaret Sanger, who founded the American Birth Control League in 1921, was also involved in the U.S. eugenics movement, which advocated, among other things, for the sterilization of the mentally incompetent. This, however, does not justify the conclusion that *all* early twentieth-century birth-control advocates favored eugenics. Such an assertion would be a logical fallacy known as a *hasty generalization.*

You should also ask whether the same facts could be interpreted in another way to support a different thesis. For example, G. Stanley Hall, an early twentieth-century American psychologist, amassed evidence that demonstrated a correlation between a woman's educational level and the number of children she had: Women who attended colleges and universities had fewer children than their less educated sisters. From these facts, he concluded that higher education caused sterility in women. A modern historian looking at the same evidence might conclude that education allowed women to become economically independent, freed them from the necessity of forming early marriages, and allowed them to pursue careers other than raising children.

Another consideration is whether the cause-and-effect relationships described in a source are legitimate. It may be true that event A happened before event B, but that does not necessarily mean that A caused B. For example, on July 20, 1969, Neil Armstrong became the first person to walk on the moon. The following winter was particularly harsh in the United States. We should not necessarily conclude, however, that the lunar landing caused a change in weather patterns. This would be a *post hoc* fallacy, from the Latin *post hoc, ergo propter hoc* (after this, therefore because of this).

In addition, you should consider how the author deals with any counterevidence. (See pp. 31 and 61 for a discussion of counterevidence.)

HOW DOES THE SOURCE COMPARE WITH OTHERS I HAVE CONSULTED? Does the source add to your knowledge of the subject? How is it different from other sources you have read? Does the author contradict or disagree with others who have written on the subject? If so, which arguments or interpretations do you find most convincing?

2b-3. Evaluating Internet sources

Internet sites that are maintained by universities, museums, government agencies, and other institutions can be a gold mine for students whose access to large research libraries is limited. Making effective use of this research tool, however, requires you to anticipate and avoid the special problems that it presents. The most significant difficulty that students encounter when trying to evaluate an Internet source is that although articles in scholarly journals and books from academic presses are carefully reviewed by other scholars in the field, anyone with the right software can post information on the Internet. Students should therefore be especially careful to determine the reliability of their Internet sources.

In attempting to evaluate an Internet source, students should first determine whether the source they are using is primary or secondary and ask the same questions they would use to evaluate a similar source in print. In addition, Internet users should consider the following:

- Is the author's identity clear, and, if so, what are his or her academic credentials? Does the author list an academic degree? Is he or she affiliated with a college or university?
- Does the author of the Web site provide evidence for his or her assertions, and does the site include source citations, bibliographies, and so on?
- Is the Web site affiliated with an academic institution, press, or journal? The Web address — or URL — can provide some clues to such affiliations. If ".edu" or ".gov" appears in the address, it has been posted by an educational or governmental institution, which may give you some confidence in the material it contains.
- Is the Web site sponsored by a particular group or organization? (Look for ".org" in the URL.) Do you know anything about the interests and concerns of the person or group that publishes the Web site?
- Does the information on the Web site coincide with what you have learned about the subject from other sources?
- Has the Web site been updated recently?
- Does the Web site contain useful links to other sites? Are the linked sites affiliated with reputable institutions or persons?

If you are still unsure if the source is reliable, it is best to consult your professor or a reference librarian.

2b-4. Looking at historical sources: An example

Much of the excitement in studying history comes from working with a wide variety of source materials. The following five primary sources (two written texts, an eyewitness account transcribed from a film, one photograph, and one cartoon) and one secondary source all pertain to the same event: the Scopes trial, one of the most famous trials of the twentieth century. Taken as a group, these sources illustrate some of the challenges — and pleasures — of working with historical sources.

In the summer of 1925, a high school teacher named John Thomas Scopes was arrested in Dayton, Tennessee, for violating the Butler Act, a state law prohibiting the teaching of Darwin's theory of evolution in public schools. Although the trial was contrived — the ACLU, which wanted to test the constitutionality of the Butler Act, had advertised that it was willing to defend anyone arrested for violating the statute, and the city fathers of Dayton, hoping to "put Dayton on the map," had asked a cooperative Scopes to play the part of defendant — the trial was nonetheless quickly dubbed "the trial of the century." Undoubtedly, the trial highlighted many of the most important social issues and intellectual conflicts in American culture in the 1920s: the relationship of science and religion, the tensions between urban and rural American culture, the rights of the majority versus those of the minority, and academic freedom versus community values. Perhaps even more important in attracting the attention of contemporaries, however, was the prominence of the lead attorneys in the trial: Clarence Darrow, the well-known champion of unpopular civil liberties causes, for the defense; and William Jennings Bryan, the "great commoner" and three-time Democratic presidential candidate, for the prosecution.

On the seventh day of the proceedings, Darrow, in an unexpected and unprecedented move, called Bryan to the stand as an "expert witness" on the Bible. Astonishingly, Bryan agreed to testify. The direct confrontation of these two larger-than-life figures provided one of the most dramatic and highly publicized moments in the trial. The following documents capture that moment.

Document 1 is a short excerpt from the trial transcripts. At this point in the proceedings, Darrow is questioning Bryan about the creation of the earth:

> [DARROW:] Do you think the earth was made in six days?
>
> [BRYAN:] Not six days of twenty-four hours.
>
> [DARROW:] Doesn't it say so?
>
> [BRYAN:] No, sir.
>
> [PROSECUTING ATTORNEY A. THOMAS] STEWART: I want to interpose another objection. What is the purpose of this examination?
>
> BRYAN: The purpose is to cast ridicule on everybody who believes in the Bible, and I am perfectly willing that the world shall know that these gentlemen have no other purpose than ridiculing every Christian who believes in the Bible.
>
> DARROW: We have the purpose of preventing bigots and ignoramuses from controlling the education of the United States and you know it, and that is all. . . .

BRYAN . . . I am simply trying to protect the word of God against the greatest atheist or agnostic in the United States! (Prolonged applause.) I want the papers to know I am not afraid to get on the stand in front of him and let him do his worst! I want the world to know! (Prolonged applause.)[3]

Document 2 is an excerpt from the *New York Times'* coverage of the seventh day of the trial, as it appeared in the paper on July 21, 1925:

So-called Fundamentalists of Tennessee sat under the trees of the Rhea County Court House lawn today listening to William J. Bryan defend his faith in the "literal inerrancy" of the Bible, and laughed. . . . The greatest crowd of the trial had come in anticipation of hearing Messrs. Bryan and Darrow speak, and it got more than it expected. It saw Darrow and Bryan in actual conflict — Mr. Darrow's rationalism in combat with Mr. Bryan's faith — and forgot for the moment that Bryan's faith was its own. . . . There was no pity for the helplessness of the believer come so suddenly and unexpectedly upon a moment when he could not reconcile statements of the bible with generally accepted facts. There was no pity for his admissions of ignorance of things boys and girls learn in high school. . . . These Tennesseans were enjoying a fight. That an ideal of a great man, a biblical scholar, an authority on religion, was being dispelled seemed to make no difference. They grinned with amusement and expectation. . . . And finally, when Mr. Bryan, pressed harder and harder by Mr. Darrow, confessed he did not believe everything in the Bible should be taken literally, the crowd howled.[4]

Document 3 is an account of the same event as it was remembered by an elderly Dayton native named Eloise Reed, who recalled her impressions of the famous confrontation between Darrow and Bryan in a recent documentary film.[5] Her brother had been a member of the high school football team that Scopes coached, and she had attended the trial as a twelve-year-old girl:

The courtyard was packed. There were not enough seats to hold all of the people and they were standing around. The

3. Jeffrey P. Moran, *The Scopes Trial: A Brief History with Documents* (Boston: Bedford/St. Martin's, 2002), 156.

4. *New York Times,* 21 July 1925, 1.

5. *The Monkey Trial,* prod. and dir. Christine Lesiak, 50 minutes, A & E Entertainment, 2000, videocassette. A transcript of the film can be found online at www.pbs.org/wgbh/amex/monkeytrial/filmmore/pt.html>.

benches had been set up all in front of the stand so we had a seat right in front of Darrow and Bryan. And I was all set to hear the great trial going on. . . . William Jennings Bryan was sitting there with a big palm fan and a handkerchief in his hand. Darrow is in his shirtsleeves with red suspenders, which he wore. He jumped up right in front of him, took hold of his red suspenders and flipped them, and said, "Do you really believe that that whale swallowed Jonah?" . . . He just kept pushing him and pushing him. You know I wanted to get up off of that bench and go up there and kick him. It was just, I imagine people out there in the audience felt the same way to make him hush. The thing was, he was attacking the Bible. Finally the judge said to him, "Well, what do you mean. You are harassing your own witness. What you are asking him has nothing to do with the issue of this trial. We want you to put a stop to it."

Document 4 is a photograph (Figure 2.1) taken during the trial; Darrow (standing) is examining Bryan (at the left of the photograph, holding a fan).[6]

Finally, Document 5 is a political cartoon (Figure 2.2) that appeared in the August 1, 1925, issue of *Judge,* a periodical published in New York from 1881 to 1939.[7] It depicts a stern Darrow (right) confronting a crying Bryan (left); the caption reads "There Ain't No Santy Claus."

Figure 2.1 Overhead view of the Scopes Trial

6. The photograph can be found on the Web at <www.law.umkc.edu/faculty/projects/ftrials/scopes/darrowcrossujpg>.

7. The cartoon first appeared in *Judge,* August 1, 1925 (vol. 89, no. 2283), 14. It can also be found on the Web at <www.law.umkc.edu/faculty/projects/Ftrials/scopes/sco_ca1.htm>.

Figure 2.2 Cartoon of Bryan and Darrow

An observant reader would notice immediately that, while the five primary sources are all contemporary records of the Scopes trial, they represent distinctive points of view regarding Bryan's personality and the impression he made on the stand at the trial. In working with these documents, then, the historian would need to determine the biases and perspectives that each source represents. How does each of these sources depict the demeanor and behavior of Bryan and Darrow? How are Bryan and Darrow depicted in the cartoon, and what does this imply about their attitudes and personalities? How do the sources portray their confrontation at the trial? How do Documents 1 through 4 depict the observers' response to Bryan's testimony? Do the sources agree on any details that would enable us to determine "what happened"? Where do the sources disagree? What is the significance of these contradictions, and what might account for them? Which of the two eyewitness accounts (Documents 2 and 3) better accords with the actual transcripts of the trial? To what extent does the *Times* reporter's status as an "outsider" give him a different perspective on events than that of

Eloise Reed, a local? Does the photograph tend to support any particular version of the event? Was the photograph published, and, if so, where? Why, and under what circumstances, did each of these accounts come to be recorded? Do these circumstances affect the degree to which we should be willing to trust them? For example, Documents 2 and 5 appeared in the *New York Times* and *Judge*, respectively. What do we know about these publications? Were they conservative or liberal? Who comprised their general readership, and what political, social, or economic groups did they represent? Where did they stand on the issues at the heart of the Scopes trial? In general, then, the student should ask: What biases are revealed in the sources? How should my awareness of these biases affect the way I read the texts and look at the cartoons and photographs? And, finally, are there any additional related sources to which these should be compared?

In *Summer for the Gods*, historian Edward J. Larson offers this description and analysis of the seventh day of the trial:

> As the inquiry departed ever further from any apparent connection to the Tennessee law against teaching evolution supposedly at issue in the trial, the prosecutor objected, "What is the purpose of this examination?" Darrow answered honestly. "We have the purpose of preventing bigots and ignoramuses from controlling the education of the United States," he declared, "and that is all." That was more than enough, for it justified his efforts to publicly debunk fundamentalist reliance on scripture as a source of knowledge about nature suitable for setting education standards. Darrow had gone to tiny Dayton, Tennessee, for precisely this purpose, with Bryan as his target. Bryan had come to defend the power of local majorities to enact a law — his law — to ban teaching about human evolution in public schools. Two hundred reporters had followed to record the epic encounter. They billed it as "the trial of the century" before it even began. . . .[8]

Later in the book, Larson returns to the same scene:

> Then, with the jury still excused, [defense attorney] Hayes called Bryan as the defense's final expert on the Bible, and the Commoner again proved cooperative. Up to this point [prosecuting attorney] Stewart had masterfully confined

8. Edward J. Larson, *Summer for the Gods* (New York, NY: Basic Books, 1997), 6.

> the proceedings and, with help from a friendly judge, controlled his wily opponents. . . . Yet Stewart could not control his impetuous co-counsel and the judge seemed eager to hear the Peerless Leader defend the faith. . . . Stewart tried to end the two-hour interrogation at least a dozen times, but Bryan refused to step down. "I am simply trying to protect the word of God against the greatest atheist or agnostic in the United States," he shouted, pounding his fist in rage. "I want the papers to know I am not afraid to get on the stand in front of him and let him do his worst." The crowd cheered this outburst and every counterthrust attempted by the Commoner. Darrow received little applause but inflicted the most jabs.[9]

While primary documents are essential to the historian's work, Larson's analysis illustrates some of the ways in which secondary sources can be useful to students in their attempts to engage in historical studies. First of all, it provides a model of how historians analyze documents (in this case, the trial transcript) and use them to reconstruct a historical event. Larson's analysis also puts the primary documents into the broader context of ongoing media interest in the trial. Moreover, he provides the reader with important information about the historical background to the events of the seventh day of the trial. He tells us, for example, that a fundamentalist interpretation of the biblical story of creation was not the sole issue of concern to the participants: Bryan wanted to defend the rights of local majorities to enact laws pertaining to education, while Darrow was concerned with intellectual and academic freedom. Similarly, we learn that the rest of the prosecution team did *not* want Bryan to take the stand and actively tried to stop the proceedings. Armed with this knowledge, the student could return to the primary sources with new questions: How did other newspapers report the events of the trial in general and the seventh day in particular? Why didn't Stewart want Bryan to testify, and why, in the face of this opposition, did Bryan insist on taking the stand? To what extent were Bryan and Darrow involved in the issues at the heart of the Scopes trial prior to the trial itself?

Reading good secondary sources, then, is not just a way to gather information. Rather, secondary sources can provide you with models for conducting your own historical research and send you back to the primary

9. Larson, 187, 190.

sources with fresh perspectives and new questions of your own.

These primary and secondary documents illustrate some of the complexity — and excitement — of the historian's craft. As you read and analyze primary sources, critique the interpretations of secondary sources, and develop historical interpretations of your own, you will gain essential critical skills.

3 *Approaching Typical Assignments in History*

The reading and writing projects assigned to you in a history course will give you opportunities to learn more about historical issues, events, and people and also to act as a historian by contributing your own ideas to the field. This section begins with a discussion of critical reading. Reading is, after all, the assignment you will encounter most frequently in your history courses. This is followed by a review of the most common types of short writing assignments you might encounter with suggestions for some general ways of approaching these assignments.

NOTE: Many professors include detailed instructions with their writing assignments. You should always read these instructions carefully, follow them closely, and ask for further explanation if you do not fully understand them. The suggestions here are meant to complement your professor's guidelines, not in any way to replace them.

3a. Reading critically

History courses typically require a great deal of reading from a wide variety of sources. If your professor has assigned a textbook, you will probably be expected to read a chapter or two each week. You may also be asked to read a variety of secondary sources, including articles from scholarly journals or books about a particular aspect of your topic. Many professors also assign primary sources, documents ranging from medieval chronicles to legal documents to newspaper accounts. (For a fuller discussion of the types of documents historians use, see 2a.) Furthermore, if you are writing a research paper, you will need to find, read, and analyze a variety of sources pertaining to your topic that are not part of the reading assigned to the whole class.

Since reading is such an important assignment, it is essential to give serious consideration to *how* you read. Reading for a history course is not like reading a novel; it is not enough to skim each page once and get the gist of the story. In fact, as you do your reading assignments, you must accomplish several tasks: You need not only to *understand* the content of what you are reading but also to *analyze* its significance, *evaluate* its usefulness, and *synthesize* all of your reading into one coherent picture of the topic you are studying. Careful and critical reading is crucial both for active and intelligent participation in class discussion and for writing effective papers. The best way to become a careful and critical reader is to become an *active* reader, constantly asking questions of the texts you are reading.

3b. Writing history papers

Aside from research papers, which will be discussed in Chapter 4, the most common writing assignments you will encounter are summaries, book and film reviews, annotated bibliographies, short essays, and historiographic essays. Each requires a slightly different approach.

3b-1. Summaries

Your professor might ask you to summarize a document, an article, or a section of a book. Since a summary does not involve a critical analysis or interpretation of historical materials, it is not a form of historical writing *per se*. However, because summarizing requires you to condense what you have read and put the author's ideas *into your own words*, it helps ensure that you have understood and digested the material. As a result, many professors find it useful for students to write summaries, particularly of complex or difficult texts. A summary (sometimes called a *précis*) should describe the author's main point, or thesis, and the key evidence used to support it. It should *not* include your critical analysis of the text. You should note, however, that when writing a summary, it is essential that the wording and turns of phrase be entirely your own and not the author's. To do otherwise is plagiarism, which is no more acceptable in a summary than in any other kind of writing. (For a detailed discussion of plagiarism and how to avoid it, see Chapter 6.)

3b-2. Book and film reviews

A book review is not the same thing as a book report, which simply summarizes the content of a book. When writing a book review, you not only report on the content of the book but also assess its strengths and weaknesses. Students sometimes feel unqualified to write a book review; after all, the author of the book is a professional historian. However, even if you cannot write from the same level of experience and knowledge as the author, you *can* write an effective review if you understand what the assignment requires.

In writing a review you do not relate only whether you liked the book; you also tell your readers *why* you liked or disliked it. It is not enough to say, "This book is interesting"; you need to explain *why* it is interesting. Similarly, it is not enough to report that you disliked a book; you must explain your reaction. Did you find the book unconvincing because the author did not supply enough evidence to support his or her assertions? Or did you disagree with the book's underlying assumptions? Incidentally, when you are writing your review, it is unnecessary to preface statements with *I think* or *in my opinion* since readers assume that as a reviewer you are expressing your own opinions.

To understand your own reaction to the book, you need to read it carefully and critically. As a critical reader, you are not passive; you should ask questions of the book and note reactions as you read. Your book review then discusses those questions and reactions. (See 3a for advice on critical reading.) Though there is no one correct way to structure a review, the following is a possible approach:

- Summarize the book and relate the author's main point, or thesis. (Somewhere early in the paper, identify the author briefly.)
- Describe the author's viewpoint and purpose for writing; note any aspects of the author's background that are important for understanding the book.

- Note the most important evidence the author presents to support his or her thesis.
- Evaluate the author's use of evidence, and describe how he or she deals with counterevidence. (See pp. 31 and 61 for a discussion of counterevidence.) Is the book's argument convincing?
- Compare this book with other books or articles you have read on the same subject.
- Conclude with a final evaluation of the book. You might discuss who would find this book useful and why.

NOTE: *Critical* does not mean negative. If a book is well written and presents an original thesis supported by convincing evidence, say so. A good book review does not have to be negative; it does have to be fair and analytical.

While historians primarily rely on written texts, film has become an increasingly important historical source. In some courses, you might use films as primary sources; for example, if you are studying racism in the early twentieth-century United States, D. W. Griffith's *The Birth of a Nation* (1915) would be a primary source. You might also use film as a secondary source. For this reason, an increasingly common writing assignment is a film review.

The suggestions provided above for writing a book review also apply to a film review. In addition, you should do the following:

- Determine whether the film is a documentary or a feature film. Who is the intended audience, and for what reason was the film made?
- If the film is a documentary, note the academic credentials of the experts who provide the commentary. If it is a feature film, determine whether the filmmaker made use of professional historians as consultants.
- Analyze the interests and concerns of the producer, director, and screenwriter. Note any other films they have produced, directed, or written that might help the viewer understand their interests and biases. In this context, it is useful to determine whether the people most responsible for the film have provided interviews or written commentary that might shed light on their work.

- Analyze the cinematic techniques that are used to convey the story. Consider whether the visual images presented in the film enhance our understanding of the issue and the period, and whether the costumes and sets accurately portray the historical reality of the period.
- If the film is based on a play or a specific text, compare the film with the original source. What elements transfer effectively to film? Are there any themes or concepts portrayed more effectively in the film than in the text? On the other hand, are there elements of the source that are eliminated or distorted in the film?
- Compare the film with other films, books, and articles on the same subject.

3b-3. Annotated bibliographies

A bibliography is a listing of books on a particular topic, usually arranged alphabetically by authors' last names. (See 7b-2 for further information on bibliographies.) In addition to providing bibliographic information, an annotated bibliography briefly summarizes each book or article and assesses its value for the topic under discussion. In writing your entries for an annotated bibliography, keep in mind the same questions you would ask while writing a book review. Remember that entries in an annotated bibliography should be relatively short; you will not be able to write a full analysis of a book or article.

Following is an example of an annotated bibliography entry:

Duus, Peter, ed. *The Japanese Discovery of America: A Brief History with Documents*. Boston: Bedford Books, 1997.

This book explores the relationship between Japan and the United States in the mid-nineteenth century, focusing on the dramatic differences between the two cultures and the uneasiness, confusion, and misunderstandings that arose from those differences. In a short introductory history, Duus discusses Japanese isolationism, the military and economic factors that led the United States to forcefully open relations with Japan, and the ways in which the Japanese observed and interpreted Americans and their culture. The main body of the text comprises a series of documents, including political pamphlets, autobiographies, eyewitness accounts, broadsheets, and prints. The inclusion of both Japanese and American views of Japan invites a comparison of mutual misunderstandings.

3b-4. History papers: General approaches

History students are most often asked to write two types of papers: short essays and research papers. Although these papers are different in some respects, they require similar approaches.

History papers usually include a narrative that recounts "what happened." Narrative is a basic element of history writing, and it is crucial that your account of past events is accurate. Nevertheless, a series of factual statements about the past, however precise they may be, does not constitute a history paper. You will not have written a history paper if you report that something (for example, the Manchu invasion of China, the death of the Aztec king Montezuma, the rise of Islam) happened. Rather, a history paper explores *how* and *why* something happened and explains its significance.

Topic and thesis

A history paper, like many other kinds of academic writing, usually takes the form of an *argument* in support of a *thesis*. A thesis is *not* a statement of fact, a question, or an opinion, although it is sometimes confused with all of these things. Neither is a thesis the same as the *topic*. The topic of your paper is simply what the essay is about. For short assignments, professors will often assign a topic, while students may be encouraged to find their own topics for longer research papers. (See 4a for advice on finding and narrowing a topic.) Rather, a thesis is a statement that reflects what you have concluded about the topic under consideration in the paper, based on a critical analysis and interpretation of the source materials you have examined. A thesis informs the reader about the *conclusions* you have reached. Moreover, a thesis is always an arguable or debatable point. In fact, the purpose of a history paper is to present the reader with enough evidence to convince him or her that your thesis is correct. As a result, the thesis is the central point to which all the information in the paper relates. As Edward Proffitt, author of *The Organized Writer,* puts it, "A paper is about its thesis and nothing else."[1]

1. Edward Proffitt, *The Organized Writer: A Brief Rhetoric* (Mountain View, Calif.: Mayfield Publishing Co., 1992), 18.

The following is the first draft of a thesis statement from a student paper on Samuel George Morton, a nineteenth-century physician and scientist who wrote several influential treatises on craniometry, the nineteenth-century science of measuring the human skull:

INEFFECTIVE THESIS

> Morton measured the size and shape of human skulls from various racial and ethnic groups, concluding that Caucasians had the largest skulls and were therefore superior to all other races.

This is not really a thesis at all. While it is an accurate *description* of what Morton did, it does not tell readers anything they couldn't learn from the most cursory reading of one of Morton's books.

Now look at the revised version of the thesis:

EFFECTIVE THESIS

> Morton and his contemporaries used his skull studies, which he said were objective and quantitative, to justify their belief in the superiority of the Caucasian race; however, a close examination of Morton's work reveals, as Stephen Jay Gould has suggested, that his supposedly scientific data were created by his own preconceived ideas about racial ranking.

This version of the thesis provides more than a simple description of what Morton did or said. Having studied Morton's works carefully, the writer has now come to a conclusion: Despite appearances to the contrary, Morton's studies were not scientific, and his procedures for collecting data were biased by his prejudices. Moreover, this thesis also tells readers why the writer thinks his topic is historically significant: Morton's views are important because they provided his contemporaries with a seemingly scientific justification for racism. Finally, this thesis statement anticipates the type of argument that will follow: The paper examines Morton's skull studies, discusses the ways in which they appear to be scientific, demonstrates the ways in which they are not scientific, and reveals the hidden biases and assumptions behind them. For all of these reasons, the revised thesis is much more effective than the draft thesis. (See pp. 56–57 for a discussion of including your thesis in the opening paragraph of your papers.)

In essence, then, when you write a paper in history, you are expected to interpret sources and, using those interpretations, to come to a conclusion about the meaning and significance of your subject. You express this conclusion in the main point, or thesis, of your paper. To support your thesis, you offer evidence from your sources. You should also respond to counterevidence, information that seems to contradict or weaken your thesis. (See pp. 31 and 61 for a discussion of counterevidence.)

Finally, you should remember that professional historians, working from the same sources, often form very different opinions about them. Thus it is unlikely that there is one correct interpretation of any topic that you will write about. You do, however, need to convince readers that your interpretation is a valid one. You will be able to do this only if you have provided *concrete evidence* — based on reliable sources — that supports your thesis and have responded honestly to opposing positions.

3b-5. Short essays

Unlike most research papers, essays are relatively brief (about five to ten pages), and the topic and text(s) are usually assigned. You might be asked, for example, to analyze a source or group of sources and respond to a specific question about them. Here is an example of a short essay assignment for a class in the history of science:

> Compare the views expressed by Nicole Oresme [a late-medieval natural philosopher] and Galileo Galilei on the role of religious beliefs in the study of the natural world.

In a different class, you might be asked to write an in-depth analysis of one text or to compare the views of two modern historians on the same issue. However different these assignments may appear to be, they all require similar responses.

ANALYZE THE ASSIGNMENT CAREFULLY. What will you need to know to write this paper? Make sure you identify and understand *all* the parts of the assignment. For the history of science example, it would not be sufficient to write a paper about Galileo using a few references to Oresme for comparison. You would need to understand what *both* Oresme and Galileo thought about the role of religious beliefs in the study of the natural world and give approximately equal weight to each in your discussion. Because the assignment asks you to compare the views of Oresme and Galileo, you would also need to understand both how their views are similar and how they differ.

You should also be careful to write about the topic that has actually been assigned. In reading Oresme and Galileo, for example, you may discover that both discuss the extent to which a natural philosopher should rely on the authority of Aristotle. Although this is an interesting issue, it is not the subject of the assignment.

CONSIDER THE SIGNIFICANCE OF THE MATERIAL. It is not enough to present a laundry list of similarities and differences or to report the contents of the texts you have read. Nor should your paper be composed of two minipapers — one on Oresme and one on Galileo — glued together. Instead, when you write a history paper, you are expected to consider the significance of the issue you are examining. In the sample assignment, the instructor's expectation is that the student will examine not only the ways the two authors are similar and different but the *meaning* of those similarities and differences. In responding to the sample assignment, you might discover, for example, that both Oresme and Galileo believe that God is the creator of the universe and the author of the natural laws that govern it. In writing the essay, you would be expected to discuss why this similarity is important. Or a comparison of the two texts might reveal that Oresme believes that the Bible can answer questions about the natural world, while Galileo argues that Scripture has no place in scientific discussions. In that case you should discuss the significance of this difference.

You should also think about the historical issue underlying the assignment. In this essay assignment, the student is asked to compare the views of Oresme, a fourteenth-century natural philosopher, with those of Galileo, who, two centuries after Oresme, became a central figure in the scientific revolution. One purpose of this assignment might be to encourage the student to think about the relationship between medieval and early modern views of the world.

CONSTRUCT AN ARGUMENT IN SUPPORT OF A THESIS. A short essay, like any paper in history, should have a thesis that is supported by evidence presented in the body of the essay. As noted earlier, your thesis reflects what you have concluded about the issue after careful reflection on the assignment and any reading that you have done for it. (See 5a-2 for further discussion of the thesis.) The student who concludes that Oresme's and Galileo's ideas are similar would write a thesis about the significance of those similarities:

> Popular descriptions of Galileo imply that he believed science and religion to be incompatible, but a comparison of his ideas with those of Nicole Oresme suggests that Galileo's ideas about God and nature were similar to the beliefs held by medieval natural philosophers.

The student who concludes that the differences between Oresme and Galileo are more significant than their similarities would write a thesis reflecting such an interpretation:

> Both Galileo and Oresme believe in God, but the similarity ends there: While Oresme sees Scripture as the ultimate font of all knowledge, Galileo dismisses it as irrelevant to the issues explored by scientists.

Note that the writers of these two theses have read the same texts and arrived at opposite conclusions, neither of which is right or wrong. What is essential is that the students support their theses with evidence taken from the texts. It is *not* enough simply to make an assertion and expect readers to agree.

RESPOND TO COUNTEREVIDENCE. Acknowledging counterevidence — information that does not support your argument — will not weaken your paper. On the contrary, if you address counterevidence effectively, you strengthen your argument by showing why it is legitimate despite information that seems to contradict it. If, for example, you wish to argue for continuity between medieval and Renaissance science, you would need to show that the similarities between Galileo's and Oresme's ideas are more significant than the differences. If you want to argue in support of the differences between the two, you might try to show that their similarities are superficial and that Galileo's rejection of Scripture as a source of knowledge about the natural world constitutes a significant change in the way people thought about science. In either case, your argument must be based on evidence and counterevidence contained in the relevant texts, not merely on your own gut feelings. (See p. 61 for further discussion of counterevidence.)

DOCUMENT YOUR PAPER. Even a short essay requires that you cite and document the sources of your information. Even if your essay is an analysis of a single source, you *must* cite that source; otherwise you will be guilty of plagiarism. (See 6b for a discussion of when to cite sources. Models for how to document various kinds of historical sources can be found in 7d.)

3b-6. Historiographic essays

Historians frequently disagree about how to interpret the events they study. For example, some historians have interpreted the Magna Carta, a charter signed by King John of England in 1215, as a revolutionary declaration of fundamental individual freedoms; others have seen it as a conservative restatement of feudal privilege. Similarly, historians interested in the same historical event might examine different sets of sources to answer the same question. In studying the causes of the French Revolution, Marxist historians might focus on economic and class issues while intellectual historians might concentrate on the impact of the writings of the philosophes (a group of French Enlightenment writers) on political thought and practice. To make students aware of debates among scholars and to acquaint them with a variety of interpretations, some instructors ask their students to write historiographic essays.

A historiographic essay is one in which you, acting as a historian, study the work of other historians. When you write a historiographic essay, you identify, compare, and evaluate the viewpoints of two or more historians writing on the same subject. Such an essay can take several forms. You might be asked, for example, to study the work of historians who lived during or near the time in which a particular event happened — for example, to explore the ways in which contemporary Chinese historians wrote about the Boxer Rebellion. A different kind of historiographic essay might require that you look at the ways in which historians have treated the same topic over time. For example, to examine how historians have treated Thomas Jefferson, you might begin with two pre–Civil War biographies — Matthew L. Davis's *Memoirs of Aaron Burr* (1836–37), which provides a scathing critique of

Jefferson, and Henry S. Randall's contrastingly positive *Life of Jefferson* (1858) — and end with the most recent studies of Jefferson. Yet another such assignment might ask you to compare the views of historians from several historical "schools" on the same event. You might, for example, be asked to compare Whig and Progressive interpretations of the American Revolution or Marxist and feminist views of the French Revolution. Historiographic essays may be short or quite lengthy. In any case, a historiographic essay focuses attention not on a historical event itself but rather on how historians have interpreted that event.

A historiographic essay combines some of the features of a book review with those of a short essay or research paper. You should begin by reading critically the texts containing historians' interpretations, keeping in mind the questions you would need to answer if you were going to write book reviews about them (see 3b-3). You should not, however, treat the historiographic essay as two or three book reviews glued together. Rather, you should synthesize your material and construct an argument in support of a thesis. The following thesis is from a student's essay on historians' interpretation of the colonial period of African history:

> Historians have held dramatically different views about the importance of European colonial rule in Africa: Marxist historians, along with others who focus on economic issues, have tended to see the colonial period as an important turning point, while cultural historians have maintained that the impact of the West on the ancient cultural traditions of Africa was superficial.

In the rest of the paper, the student supports the thesis as he or she would do in any other history paper.

3b-7. Revising and editing your paper

One of the biggest mistakes that students make with any writing assignment is to leave themselves too little time to revise and edit their work. Although some students take a rather perverse pride in their ability to write a passable paper the night before it is due, the resulting work is never of the highest caliber and usually bears the hallmarks of careless writing: sloppy mistakes in reasoning, awkward constructions, poor word choice, lack of clear organization, and, of course, spelling and grammar mistakes. To write an effective history paper, you *must* allow yourself time to revise your paper.

When you revise, you need to read your paper critically, as if it were someone else's work. (For advice on critical reading, see 3a.) You should read for logic and clarity. You should make sure that your evidence is sufficient and that it supports your thesis. You should also look for wordiness and awkward sentence structure, for repetition and cliché. You must be willing to rearrange the order of material, do additional research to support weak points in your argument, and even change your entire thesis, if necessary. Obviously, you need to allow plenty of time for this part of the writing process, which may involve several drafts of the paper.

GRAMMAR AND SPELL CHECKERS. Running the spell and grammar checkers on your computer is *not* the same as revising your paper. You should, of course, use both of these tools if they are available to you. However, running the spell checker will not pick up incorrectly used homophones (for example, *their, there,* and *they're*) or other words spelled correctly but used incorrectly. Nor should you rely on your grammar checker to catch every mistake. Always edit and proofread the final copy of your paper carefully; your instructor will not look kindly on a paper that is full of typographical, grammatical, and spelling errors.

3c. Taking history exams

History exams can follow many different formats. Two of the most typical kinds of questions found on history exams are essays, in which you are asked to discuss a particular historical question or issue in some detail, and identifications, in which you are asked to briefly identify and note the significance of an important person, place, or event.

3c-1. Preparing for an exam

The best preparation for an exam does not begin the day, or even the week, before the exam but takes place throughout the semester. Careful reading of the texts and periodic review of your notes will ensure that you have a firm grasp of the material come exam time.

Throughout the semester, you should do the following:

- Attend class regularly, and take good notes. It is not necessary to write down *everything* your professor says. When taking notes, you should listen for the professor's *main points* and note the evidence that he or she gives to support those points. (You will discover that your professor's lectures usually follow the same format as a good essay.) Follow the same suggestions for a discussion class; your classmates will often make important points about the material you are studying.
- Review your notes regularly, preferably after each class. If you review your notes while the class is fresh in your mind, it will be easier for you to notice places where the notes are unclear. Mark these places, and clarify confusing points as soon as possible, either by researching the issue yourself or by asking your professor.
- As you read your texts and review your class notes, it is useful to make a running list of significant persons, places, events, and concepts, along with a brief description of why they are important and, for terms with which you are unfamiliar, a definition. This will not only ensure that you understand the key ideas in the material you are studying, but will also be particularly useful if your exam for the course includes an identification section. How do you know which items to include on this list? Some will be obvious; if you are taking a course called "The Age of Dictators," it would be a good thing to be able to identify Hitler, Mussolini, and Stalin. In cases in which the importance of a person or an idea is not so obvious, look for other clues: words that are italicized in your texts; concepts that recur in several of your readings; and terms, events, or people that your professor has highlighted for you or written on the board.
- Refer to your syllabus throughout the semester. Many professors provide detailed syllabi that state the themes for each section of the course. Use this as a guide for your own studying and thinking about the course material.
- Take careful notes on the material you are reading for the course. Keep in mind that simply copying long sections from your texts is not very useful in

ensuring that you have understood the material. It will be much more useful for you to take notes in the form of summaries (see 3b-2 for a fuller discussion).

- If one is not assigned for the course, consider keeping an academic journal. In your journal, record important points about the material you are reading, any questions you want to answer or issues you would like to raise, important ideas suggested by class discussions, and so on. You can use the journal to track your growing knowledge of the material you are studying.

The week before the exam, you should do the following:

- Review your notes, syllabus, and texts. Identify the most important themes and issues of the course, and assemble the evidence that clarifies those themes.
- Imagine that you are the professor faced with the task of setting the exam for this course. What questions would you ask? Framing your own exam questions and answering them can be a useful way of organizing your thoughts.

3c-2. Taking an essay exam

The essays you write for an exam will necessarily be shorter than the papers you write for your course, but they should follow the same basic format. In other words, an exam essay should begin with a thesis, stated clearly in the first paragraph, followed by several paragraphs in which you provide evidence supporting your thesis, and end with a conclusion. The difficulty, of course, is that you will be writing *this* essay under pressure, in a limited period of time, and without the opportunity to check the accuracy of your data.

Here are some suggestions for writing a successful essay on a history exam.

BEFORE YOU WRITE. *Do not begin to write right away.* This is probably the biggest mistake that students make in essay exams. Before you write, do the following:

- Read the exam carefully. Make sure you understand what each question is really asking. You will not gain points by scribbling down everything you know about the development of Chinese politics from the tenth through the fifteenth century when the question asks you to discuss the impact of the Mongol invasion in 1260.

- If you are offered a choice, make sure you answer the question you can answer best. This may not always be the one you are drawn to first. One great insight about the significance of the Treaty of Waitangi will not be enough to write a good essay about Maori-British relations in nineteenth-century New Zealand. Be sure that you can cite several pieces of evidence in support of your thesis.
- Take the time to organize your thoughts. Jot down a quick outline for your essay, stating the thesis and listing the evidence you will provide to support that thesis.

WRITING THE ESSAY. Once you are ready to write, your essay should follow the same format as any other history essay:

- Begin by stating your thesis. *Do not* waste time restating the question: Your professor knows what he or she asked.
- Cite the evidence that supports your thesis. If you are aware of any counterevidence, make sure you discuss it. (See pp. 31 and 61 for a discussion of counterevidence and how to deal with it.)
- Be sure you *stick to the point.* Do not go off on interesting tangents that are irrelevant to the question. Referring frequently to your outline will help you keep on track.
- Tie your essay together by stating your conclusions.

3c-3. Answering identification questions

Professors often use identification questions as a way of testing your basic understanding of the material covered in the course. You may be asked to identify people, places, or events, or to define important concepts. If, as suggested above, you have kept a running list of significant individuals, events, and terms, you probably will not be surprised by any of the items in the identification section of your test.

When answering identification questions, it is important to *read the directions carefully*. Students tend to make one of two mistakes in answering identification questions. On the one hand, they may produce answers that are too detailed. The response to an identification question should not be a full-blown four-page essay. So, how much should you write? Often, your professor will tell you how long your response should be; you might, for example, be asked to answer in one sentence or to write a three to four-sentence paragraph. The number of points an identification answer is worth also provides a clue to how much time you should spend writing your response. If your exam includes an essay worth 50 points, and ten identifications worth 5 points each, you obviously should not spend thirty minutes on one identification.

The second, opposite mistake is to write too little. Again, if each identification is worth 5 points, identifying Anne Boleyn as "an English queen" is clearly not enough; dozens of people can be identified as English queens. Rather, your answer should be specific enough to identify the individual person, event, or concept. Thus, a more successful response to an identification question on Anne Boleyn would include the information that she was the second wife of Henry VIII and the mother of Queen Elizabeth I. Moreover, identification questions may ask you to go one step further by noting the significance of the person, event, or concept. Sometimes, this expectation is spelled out in the directions; you are instructed to "identify and *explain the significance of* the following." At other times, the suggested length of your answer provides the clue; if you are asked to write three to four sentences, you will need to provide more than a minimal identification. In this instance, thinking about why your professor has asked you to identify particular persons, events, or concepts will help you to formulate your answer.

4
Writing a Research Paper

A research paper, like a short essay, usually takes the form of an argument with a thesis supported by evidence. It is different from a short essay, however, in several ways. A research paper is more substantial, usually at least fifteen pages and often much longer. More important, a research paper requires that you supplement assigned readings for the course with information from the library and other sources.

Your instructor might assign a specific research topic, or the choice might be left entirely up to you. Most often, you will be given some choice within a general area. The syllabus for a course with a research paper might, for example, include a statement like this in its list of course requirements:

> Research paper on any topic covered in the course, chosen in consultation with me. Your paper should be 15–18 pages and is worth 40% of the final grade.

Students often find such assignments intimidating and may secretly yearn for an assigned subject; it often seems easier to write about a topic that holds no interest for you than to face the task of defining your own area of investigation. However, when you choose your own research topic, you are engaged in the practice of history at a much more sophisticated level. You are, in fact, doing the same work that a professional historian does: answering the questions *you yourself* have posed about a subject that you find compelling or problematic. The research paper, then, is both challenging and enormously exciting. It allows you, while still a student, to undertake original research and, perhaps, even discover something new.

Consider the following advice before you begin a research project.

4a. Thinking about your topic

A research paper represents a significant investment of time and effort. Before you begin, therefore, you should think carefully not only about your interests but also about the feasibility of your proposed topic.

CHOOSE A SUBJECT THAT INTERESTS YOU. Start with the texts assigned for your class, and find a general area that appeals to you. As you begin, your subject can be relatively broad — for example, "slavery and the Civil War." You will not know what problems, issues, and questions exist within the larger framework of the broad topic until you familiarize yourself with the general subject.

CONSIDER THE AVAILABILITY OF SOURCES. In deciding on a topic, you should consider what sources are available to you in your own college or university library. For example, you might decide that it would be interesting to examine the views of artisans during the French Revolution, but if you cannot obtain enough sources of information on this subject, this will not be a workable topic.

If your own institution's holdings are limited, you may be able to supplement them by borrowing materials from nearby colleges and universities or from more distant sources through interlibrary loan. Don't overlook public libraries, especially in larger urban centers; many have surprisingly good holdings. And, of course, you may be able to get sources over the Internet (see 4b-1 for more on using Internet sources). Nevertheless, it is certainly easier to begin with a topic for which your own library has a reasonable number of sources.

Similarly, you should consider whether the sources for the topic in which you are interested are written in a language that you can read fluently. In the example cited above, for example, you might find that your library has a large collection of sources on artisans in revolutionary France — in French. In this case, consider whether your command of the language is sufficient for the research you hope to pursue.

NARROW YOUR SUBJECT DOWN TO A WORKABLE TOPIC. Once you have begun to gather materials related to your area of interest, you will need to narrow your subject down to a workable topic. After all, you will not be able to write effectively on a broad topic like "slavery and the Civil War" within the length of a typical research paper.

Narrowing your topic to one that is feasible always begins with reading; however, simply reading everything you can find about slavery and the Civil War will *not* help you find a suitable research topic. Your reading must be active, not passive. In other words, you must be actively engaged in a dialogue with the texts you are reading, constantly asking questions that direct your reading.

A history paper usually begins with a question, and you can begin to narrow your broad subject by rephrasing your topic as a series of questions. What is it that you want to know about "slavery and the Civil War"? Are you interested in the role of abolitionists in the war? In the events and ideas that led up to the Emancipation Proclamation? In what slaves thought about the war? List those questions, and try to answer them as you read. As you begin to answer some of your initial questions, you will gain a deeper knowledge of your subject, and more detailed questions will arise: What role did freed slaves play in Union regiments? How were black soldiers treated by their white commanders? If you read actively in this way, you will discover which questions have been thoroughly discussed and which are less well studied. You will find the areas in which historians have reached consensus and questions that are still the subject of debate. Ultimately, you may even find an area where you feel you can say something both interesting and original. At this point in the process of narrowing your topic, you will be able to generate the thesis that will drive your research paper. (For a more detailed discussion of the thesis, see 5a-2.)

WRITE AS YOU READ. Most scholars would agree that reading and writing are interactive processes. The writing that you do while reading can take many different forms. If you own some of the books you are using for your paper, or if you have made photocopies of some of the important materials you will be using, you might want to write directly on the text, underlining important points and writing comments in the margins. Develop your own code for marginal notation so that you will be able to identify arguments that you find questionable, insights that you find important, or words that you need to define. You might also find it useful to write summaries of your reading to ensure that you have understood the material (see 3b-1 for advice on summaries). It is also useful to copy out, in quotation marks, any particularly striking phrases or statements that you might want to quote directly in your work. (When you do this, always make sure to write out the full bibliographic citation in your notes.) For a lengthy project, you might even consider keeping a reading journal, in which you can record any ideas, insights, or questions that occur to you as you read. In any case, writing will help you clarify your thoughts about what you are reading and provide direction for your research.

START YOUR RESEARCH EARLY. The day you receive the assignment is not too soon to begin your research. The importance of starting early becomes obvious once you realize that Internet sources, while often very useful and readily available, are *not* sufficient for a research paper. You will need to consult books, journal articles, and other print materials. Therefore, it is always safest to anticipate problems in gathering your sources: other people may have borrowed the books you need, or you may have to travel to other libraries to use their collections. If you are interested in a topic for which your own library has only limited sources, you might be able to borrow books from other colleges and universities on interlibrary loan. But to ensure that you get your books in time, you will need to make your request early.

4b. Conducting research

A great deal of the work you do in writing a research paper happens *before* you begin to write your first draft. This section deals with the research skills that you will need to master to make the most of the wealth of material available to you.

BEGIN BY CONSULTING YOUR PROFESSOR. Although a research paper may seem daunting to you, you should remember that your professor has had a great deal of experience in conducting research and writing papers and is intimately familiar with the research produced by other historians. Take advantage of this expertise by utilizing office hours, chat rooms, Web sites, and other forums for consulting your professor. He or she will be delighted by your interest and will be happy to point you in a number of potentially fruitful directions. Ask your professor to recommend books and articles on your topic, and make sure you consult these at the outset of your research. Then, as you begin to conduct your own search for materials, you can use their notes and bibliographies as a guide for gathering additional material. Your professor can also direct you to the most important scholarly journals in the field you are researching.

GENERATE A WORKING BIBLIOGRAPHY. The next step in beginning your research paper is to generate a working bibliography. You should start your search in the library. The amount of material you find, even from a brief examination of your library's holdings, may at first seem overwhelming. How do you know which of the many books and journal articles that your library contains are the most useful to you? Where should you start? In addition to the books and articles recommended by your professor, it is often useful to consult articles in appropriate scholarly journals. Start with the most recently published articles first; they frequently contain an overview of the scholarship to date and provide references to other important books and articles. Books are, of course, another important source for research papers. When trying to decide whether a book will be useful, you should consider the points raised in Chapter 2 on evaluating sources. In addition, you should ask the following questions:

- Was the book published by an academic or popular press?
- Does the book contain complete footnotes, bibliography, and other scholarly apparatus that identifies it as a serious academic work?
- Has the book been reviewed by any scholarly journals? Were the reviews favorable?

If the book passes these tests, read the introduction and conclusion, and glance over the table of contents to determine whether it contains material pertinent to your topic; it may be a wonderful book, but it won't be helpful if it takes you off on a tangent.

Finally, keep in mind that librarians are also extremely helpful in tracking down both print and Internet materials. Invaluable and often overlooked resources are reference librarians, who can direct you to important journals, bibliographies, book reviews, and other research tools. Reference librarians can also teach you how to search the online catalog by using keywords to find recent books and journal articles in your library's collection. If your library has a card catalog, be sure to check it as well; some college libraries are still in the process of computerizing their holdings, and you may overlook important sources if you rely solely on the online catalog. You may also be able to use your library's computer to search the holdings of nearby affiliated libraries; and, of course, you can conduct an Internet search as well.

NOTE: Do not make generating a bibliography an end in itself. You still need to read the books and articles you have found! Your final bibliography should include only the materials you have read and found useful in writing your paper.

USE BOTH PRIMARY AND SECONDARY SOURCES. A good research paper contains references to a variety of sources. You will need to consult primary sources (letters, diaries, original documents, and so on) from the period you are studying. You will also need to consult secondary sources to become familiar with the ways in which other historians have interpreted this material. Your secondary sources should reflect a balance of materials. While books are valuable sources, you should not confine your research to books; important recent research is often found in articles in scholarly journals. (See Appendix B for guidance in researching primary and secondary sources.) Finally, you should be especially careful to note that Internet sources, while often quite useful, are not sufficient for a research paper. In general, then, you should consult both primary and secondary sources, and aim for a balance between books and articles.

USE NONWRITTEN MATERIALS WHERE APPROPRIATE. Although much of the work you do in an undergraduate history course will center on the reading and interpretation of written sources, historians also use a wide variety of nonwritten sources in their work. The following may be useful to you in researching and writing your paper:

- *Maps* are especially useful when you are trying to explain geographical relationships, such as the movements of troops during a battle or the changes in the national boundaries of a particular area over time.

- *Graphs and charts* are useful for illustrating statistical information, such as rates of marriages, births, or deaths and changes in per capita income over a particular period of time.
- *Photographs, cartoons,* and other illustrations can provide evidence that may support or contradict the written sources, or may provide a unique perspective on events.
- *Diagrams,* such as a sketch of the west portal of Chartres cathedral or architectural plans illustrating the floor plan and elevation of the Empire State Building, can help the reader understand how parts are related to a larger whole.

If you consult nonwritten material in your research or use it in your paper, you must cite it and provide complete bibliographical information, just as you would for any written source.

4b-1. Conducting an Internet search

The Internet offers countless possibilities for research. Due to the rapid expansion of the Internet, the amount of material available to any individual student has multiplied exponentially. The availability of information on the Internet is not, however, without drawbacks. Virtually anyone with a computer, a modem, and the right software can create a Web site. As a result, many Web sites are useless for serious research. (For help with evaluating Internet sources, see 2b-3.) Nonetheless, the Internet is a worthwhile tool for research. This section will introduce you to a few online research techniques that can make your Internet searches more effective.

When you look for information on the Internet, you will usually use either a *directory* or a *search engine.* Both of these tools are useful, but they are not the same and require different methods to be used effectively.

USING DIRECTORIES AND SEARCH ENGINES. A *directory* offers a list of categories with increasingly specialized subcategories. A typical directory, like Yahoo!, begins with a list of broad general categories that contains a number of subcategories. For instance, under the general category "Social Sciences" you will find the subcategory "History." Clicking on "History," you are invited to search by "Region," "Subject," or "Time Period" or by a number of special subcategories, including "Archives," "Oral History," and "Psychohistory." As you click through the subsequent levels of the directory, the topics become more and more specific.

Some difficulties are associated with using directories. For example, if you go to the Yahoo! directory and click on the broad category "Arts and Humanities," you will not find "History." However, if you click on "Arts and Humanities" and then click on "Humanities," you *will* find "History" as a subcategory. In general, then, when you search using a directory, you should think creatively about the categories with which your topic might be associated. If you don't find your topic on the first try, go back and try a different category until you find what you are looking for. It may not be possible to find a category that matches your topic exactly. Instead, look for the category that *best* matches your topic.

A *search engine* works somewhat differently from a directory. From your Internet server, you can access several search engines such as Excite!, HotBot, AltaVista, Lycos, Google, and Infoseek. To look for a topic using a search engine, you enter a word or group of words into the "Search" box and click on the appropriate command ("Search Now," "Go," "Submit," and so on). The search engine then searches its database and generates a list of sources that contain the word or words you searched for. A different type of search engine is a **metasearch engine** such as MetaCrawler and InferenceFind. These engines will run your search terms through several search engines at once (see Figure 4.1).

NOTE: Many search engines include an "advanced search" feature, which allows you to use the engine more effectively to find a specific topic. Since each search engine is different, you should refer to the instructions each one provides on how to conduct an advanced search.

The success of such a search depends heavily on two things: you must choose the correct word or words for your search, and you must be willing to conduct several searches using alternative words (entering "Middle Ages" will turn up a different list than the one generated by entering "medieval"). Moreover, the search engine is not

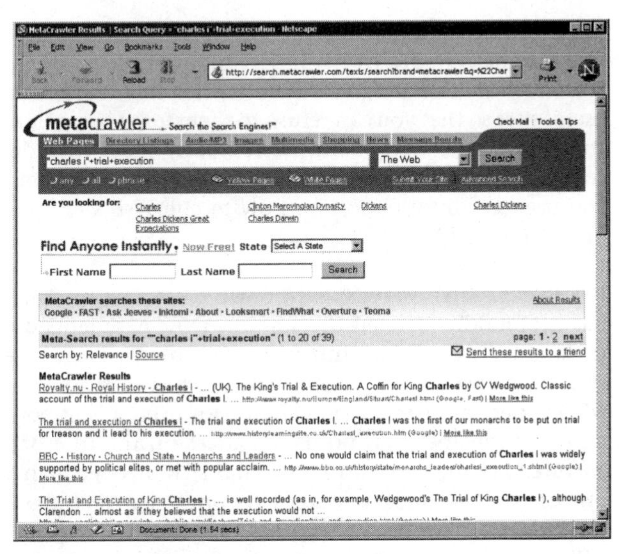

Figure 4.1 MetaCrawler, a metasearch engine

selective; it will list *every* source it finds, regardless of whether that source is relevant to your topic. For example, in writing a paper on the development of the papacy, you might search under "college of cardinals." Using a popular search engine, these keywords produced several promising sources — and also an article from the *Athens Daily Review* on the Trinity Valley Community College Cardinals football team of Athens, Texas. Second, you should never limit your search to one search engine. It is commonly assumed that search engines search the Internet: They *do not.* Rather, they search a *database.* Since each search engine uses a different database, it is essential to use several search engines for the best possible results.

Finally, the Internet provides a valuable research tool in the form of *hyperlinks* (or *links*). When you find a useful site, you will notice that some of the words for key ideas, people, and events appear in a color other than black or are underlined. These words indicate links. By clicking on a link, you can connect to other Web pages on the same subject. Thus, you can use links, just as you can use the notes and bibliography in a printed text, to find additional material. The presence of reputable, useful, and current links is also a good indication of the worthiness of a site. (For more on evaluating Internet sources, see 2b-3.)

NOTE: The results of an Internet search will probably contain many more irrelevant items than useful ones. While you are searching, it is therefore helpful to *bookmark* useful sites so that you can return to them for more careful study at a later date. Your bibliography must include complete bibliographical information about any Web sites you use. (For information on how to cite Web sites, see pp. 98 and 112.)

USE BOTH PRINT AND INTERNET SOURCES. The Internet has profoundly affected the ways in which students do research. Through the Internet, students in even the smallest colleges in the most isolated settings can access a wide variety of historical materials. However, it is important to remember that primary sources on the Internet are often not the best editions (see p. 11). Moreover, many primary and secondary sources are not yet available on the Internet. Students who rely solely on electronic media will miss many fundamental and indispensable sources. It is vital, therefore, that you consult both electronic and print sources in your research.

4c. Taking effective research notes

Your final paper will only be as good as the notes you take. There is no right or wrong way to take notes for a research paper. Many people favor index cards, which can be arranged and rearranged easily. Others prefer to use notebooks or legal pads. If you have a laptop computer, you may wish to type your notes directly into an electronic file. This can be especially useful if you use a word processing program with a global search function so that you can use the search command to find keywords quickly wherever they appear in your notes. But whatever method you use, there are several things you can do to make your note taking more effective.

ALWAYS RECORD COMPLETE BIBLIOGRAPHIC INFORMATION FOR ANY SOURCE YOU CONSULT. Nothing is more frustrating than to return all your books to the library, only to discover that you are missing authors' names, dates of publication, or other information you will need for your bibliography. (See 7d for a description of the elements that constitute "complete bibliographic information.") If you have not written many academic papers, you may find it difficult to remember all of these elements; therefore, while doing your research, you may want to keep this guide handy. Or you may find it useful to list the information you need to record on an index card that you can carry with you.)

TAKE MOST OF YOUR NOTES IN THE FORM OF SUMMARIES. If you take notes word for word from your source, you are simply acting as a human photocopier. Your goal should be to digest the information presented in your sources and make it your own. It is therefore much more useful to read carefully and thoughtfully, close the book, and summarize in your own words the section you have read. Then compare your summary with the original, noting any important points that you missed or anything that you misunderstood. At this point, you should also check carefully to make sure that you have not inadvertently taken any words or phrases directly from the original text. This type of note taking not only will ensure that you really understand the material but also will help you avoid plagiarism.

COPY QUOTATIONS ACCURATELY. If you do decide to quote directly from a source, make sure you copy the words and punctuation of your source exactly, and always use quotation marks so that you will know it is a direct quote when you return to your notes. Do not try to improve the wording of the original or correct the spelling or grammar. You may, however, alert your readers to an error in spelling or grammar by recording the error as it appears in the source and then noting the mistake by adding the Latin word *sic* in brackets, as follows: "Do not correct mispelled [sic] words."

DOCUMENT YOUR SOURCES. For a research paper, your professor will expect complete and accurate documentation of your sources. (See Chapter 7 for information on documentation.) Even if you are summarizing, you must note the source of your information and cite the source in your paper to avoid plagiarism. (See Chapter 6 for a fuller discussion of avoiding plagiarism.)

AVOID THE MISCONCEPTION THAT "TO PHOTOCOPY IS TO KNOW." Photocopying material on your topic is no substitute for reading and understanding it. Photocopying doesn't save time; in fact, it's often a time waster.

Eventually, you will have to read and interpret the photocopied material, and when you do, you may notice that you have copied irrelevant material and missed important information.

4d. Developing a working thesis

The role the thesis plays in a history paper has already been discussed in some detail in Chapter 3. In a research paper, where the writer has to pose his or her own historical questions and conduct significant independent research, the role of the thesis is particularly crucial. All of the preliminary writing that you do for your research paper — listing questions, taking notes, jotting down ideas, and so on — is intended to stimulate and clarify your thinking and thereby help you narrow your initial broad interests into a workable paper topic. The result of all of this thinking and reading and writing is the generation of a *working thesis*: a single sentence in which you state what you have concluded about your topic. It is this thesis that provides the focus toward which the entire paper is directed; everything you include in a research paper should provide evidence to support the thesis you have put forward.

In developing a working thesis, it is useful to keep in mind that a thesis is not a question, a statement of fact, a description of the paper topic, or a statement of opinion. Thus, although historians begin their research with a question or series of questions in mind, and although asking questions plays a central role in the processes of reading critically, evaluating evidence, and narrowing the focus of the paper, a question is not, in itself, a thesis. (The following question is not a thesis: "Why were Mohandas Gandhi's methods successful in the movement to achieve Indian independence from Great Britain?") Similarly, while historians deal in factual information about the past, a "fact," however interesting, is simply a piece of data. (The following statement is not a thesis: "Mohandas Gandhi led the movement by which India achieved independence from Britain.") Moreover, although your reader should not have to guess what your paper is about, the thesis must do more than announce your subject or the purpose for which you are writing. (The following sentence is not a thesis: "This paper is about the role of nonviolent resistance in the Indian independence movement." Nor is "The purpose of this paper is to describe the methods Mohandas Gandhi used to gain Indian independence from Great Britain.") Finally, although a thesis statement must reflect what you have concluded, it cannot be a simple statement of belief or preference. (The following assertion is not a thesis: "Mohandas Gandhi is my favorite political leader of the twentieth century.")

A thesis is a statement that reflects what the author has concluded about the topic of the paper; it is a product of the thinking, reading, and writing that has occurred in the process of doing research. (The following sentence *is* a thesis: "Through his acts of civil disobedience, Mohandas Gandhi succeeded in indicting British colonial policy in the court of public opinion; his nonviolent resistance to British rule in India proved to be a weapon that the British could not effectively combat.")

NOTE: As stated above, the thesis at this stage in the production of a research paper is a *working thesis*; it is the position you have come to at this point in the work. However, as you begin to organize your notes and write the paper itself, it is important to remain flexible. As you write, you will probably find that you need to do some additional research. As you do this research, you may find new information or see old information in new ways, which, in turn, may require you to modify your thesis. Willingness to modify your thesis, and to allow your research to dictate your thesis, is the hallmark of a good historian.

4e. Making an outline

Once you know what argument you wish to make and have stated it in a working thesis, it is useful to sketch out the body of your paper in the form of an outline.

The most important function of an outline is to provide a guide that notes the points you wish to cover and the order in which you plan to cover them. A good outline will help you present the evidence that supports your thesis as a convincing argument.

Some students have been trained to write formal outlines with roman numerals and various subheadings. If this method works for you, by all means use it. However, many students find formal outlines too constraining and prefer instead to write a less formal outline.

You might begin an informal outline by writing down the main points you want to discuss. These will form the topic sentences of paragraphs. Underneath each main point, list the evidence that supports it. Outlining your paper in this way will reveal any points that require additional evidence. It will also help ensure that your evidence is organized in a logical and orderly manner and that each idea is connected to those that precede and follow it.

NOTE: Remember that an outline is a *tool*. As you continue to think and write about your subject, you may discover new material or change your mind about the significance of certain material. You may even change your thesis (which is why your thesis at this stage is a *working* thesis rather than a final one). When this happens, you must be willing to revise your outline too.

4f. Revising your research paper

A research paper is a complex project. You need to analyze your sources, synthesize information, organize your thoughts, and present them in a coherent and persuasive manner. As with a short essay, you must construct an argument with a thesis and supporting evidence, but in the case of a research paper, you will need to analyze and synthesize much more material. You will probably have more counterevidence to address as well. It is unrealistic to expect that one or two drafts will be sufficient to do justice to the project. Give yourself time to revise your writing.

Obviously, a research paper represents a significant commitment of time, effort, and intellect. Nonetheless, the rewards are equally great, for it is in the research paper that students can experience the pleasures of truly original interpretation and discovery.

5
Following Conventions of Writing in History

Each academic discipline has its own practices, or conventions, that people writing in the discipline follow when engaged in a scholarly dialogue. These conventions are not hard-and-fast rules, but following them will make it easier for you to participate in an academic conversation in your field. Moreover, many historians are excellent stylists. Your instructor will pay attention to your writing, so your attempts to learn and follow the conventions of the discipline will be noticed — and worth the effort. This section first looks at general conventions of writing history papers and then turns to concerns of word choice and grammar.

5a. Considering the whole paper

Surrounded by books, photocopies, and printouts, and faced with piles of notes, it is sometimes difficult for students to know how to organize their ideas and research into an effective paper that respects the conventions established for historical writing. In considering the whole paper, it is important to keep two general principles in sight. First, historical writing describes the lives, beliefs, and practices of real people; respecting those people is a fundamental principle of historical writing. Second, history papers, like other academic writing, include an introduction, a body, and a conclusion; in each of these sections, historians expect to find specific elements. Learning the conventions that govern your relationship to your subject and the elements of historical writing will enable you to be an active participant in historical conversation.

5a-1. Your relationship to your subject

When you write a history paper, you are forming a relationship of sorts with real people and events whose integrity must be respected. It is useful to keep in mind several conventions historians have established for such relationships.

RESPECT YOUR SUBJECT. The people who lived in the past were not necessarily more ignorant or cruel (or, conversely, more innocent or moral) than we are. It is condescending, for example, to suggest that any intelligent or insightful person was "ahead of his or her time" (suggesting, of course, that he or she thought the same way we do).

DO NOT GENERALIZE. Remember that groups are formed of individuals. Do not assume that everyone who lived in the past believed the same things or behaved the same way. Avoid broad generalizations, such as "the Middle Ages was an age of faith." At best, such statements are clichés. More often than not, they are also wrong.

AVOID ANACHRONISMS. An anachronistic statement is one in which an idea, event, person, or thing is represented in a way that is not consistent with its proper historical time. For example, "Despite the fact that bubonic plague can be controlled with antibiotics, medieval physicians treated their patients with ineffective folk remedies." This sentence includes two anachronisms. First, although antibiotics are effective against bubonic plague, they had not yet been discovered in the fourteenth century; it is anachronistic to mention them in a discussion of the Middle Ages. Second, it is anachronistic to judge medieval medicine by modern standards. A more effective discus-sion of the medieval response to the bubonic plague would focus on fourteenth-century knowledge about health and disease, theories of contagion, and sanitation practices.

In short, you should not import the values, beliefs, and practices of the present into the past. Try to understand the people and events of the past in their own contexts.

BE AWARE OF YOUR OWN BIASES. We naturally choose to write about subjects that interest us. Historians should not, however, let their own concerns and biases direct the way they interpret the past. A student of early modern

Europe, for example, might be dismayed by the legal, social, and economic limitations placed on women in that period. Reproaching sixteenth-century men for being "selfish and chauvinistic" might forcefully express such a student's sense of indignation about what appears to modern eyes as unjust, but it is not a useful approach for the historian, who tries to understand the viewpoints of people in the past in the social context of the period under study.

5a-2. The introduction and thesis

The introductory paragraph of your paper is in many ways the most important one and, therefore, the most difficult to write. In your introduction, you must (1) let your readers know what your paper is about, (2) put the topic of your paper into context, and (3) state your thesis — the position you are going to take on the topic. You must also attract your readers' attention and interest. The opening paragraph, then, has to frame the rest of the paper, and it has to make readers want to continue reading.

There is no magic formula for writing an effective first paragraph. You should, however, keep these conventions in mind.

DO NOT OPEN WITH A GLOBAL STATEMENT. Unsure of how to start, many students begin their papers with phrases like "Throughout history" or "From the beginning of time" or "People have always wondered about . . . " You should avoid broad generalizations like these. First, you cannot prove that they are true: How do you know what people have always thought or done? Second, these statements are so broad that they are virtually meaningless; they offer no specific points or details to interest readers. Finally, such statements are so general that they give readers no clue about the subject of your paper. In general, it is much more effective to begin with material that is specific to your topic.

For example, the following opening sentence comes from a student's first draft of a paper on William Harvey, the seventeenth-century physician who discovered the circulation of blood:

> **INEFFECTIVE**
>
> From ancient times, people have always been interested in the human body and how it works.

Although, strictly speaking, there is nothing wrong with this sentence, it is not a particularly effective opening. For one thing, it is such a general statement that readers will be inclined to ask, "So what?" In addition, it gives readers no indication of what the paper is about. Will the essay examine ancient Greek medical theory? Chinese acupuncture? Sex education in twentieth-century American schools?

In revising the sentence, the student eliminated the general statement altogether and began instead with a description of the intellectual context of Harvey's work:

> **EFFECTIVE**
>
> For the scholars and physicians of seventeenth-century Europe, observation and experimentation began to replace authoritative texts as the most important source of information about human anatomy and physiology.

From this short sentence, readers learn four things about the subject of the paper: the time frame of the discussion (the seventeenth century), the place (Europe), the people involved (scholars and physicians), and the topic (the relationship between authority and experience in the study of human physiology). Readers' curiosity is also piqued by the questions implied in the opening statement: Why did experimentation begin to replace authoritative texts? Was this change a subject of controversy? Who was involved? How did this change in method affect the science of biology and the practice of medicine? In other words, this opening sentence makes readers want to continue reading; they want to know the author's thesis.

INCLUDE YOUR THESIS IN THE FIRST PARAGRAPH. If your opening sentence has been effective, it will make your readers want to know the main point of your paper, which you will state in the *thesis*. The thesis is the heart of your paper. It reflects the conclusion you have reached about your subject as a result of your research and analysis, and provides the focal point for the rest of the paper, in which you present the evidence and arguments that support your thesis. As you read works by professional historians, you may notice that the introductions to journal articles or books may be long, even several paragraphs, and the author's thesis may appear anywhere within it. Until you become skilled in writing about history, however, it is best to keep your introduction short and to state your thesis in the first paragraph. (For a discussion of the thesis, see sections 3b and 4d.)

The following example is the first draft of the introduction for the paper on Harvey:

INEFFECTIVE

From ancient times, people have always been interested in the human body and how it works. Harvey was a seventeenth-century physician who performed many experiments. He discovered the circulation of the blood.

This draft begins with the ineffective opening sentence we looked at above. The "thesis statement" that follows isn't really a thesis at all; it is simply a statement of fact. Moreover, there is no clear connection established between the ideas contained in the opening sentence and Harvey. From this first paragraph, a reader would have no idea what the paper was about, what its central point might be, or what to expect in the pages that follow.

In the final version of this introductory paragraph, the student has used the revised opening sentence and incorporated a more effective thesis, which is underlined here:

EFFECTIVE

For the scholars and physicians of seventeenth-century Europe, observations and experimentation began to replace authoritative texts as the most important source of information about human anatomy and physiology. This trend is clearly illustrated in the work of William Harvey, who designed controlled experiments to measure blood flow. <u>However, Harvey was not led to his revolutionary discovery of the circulation of the blood by these experiments alone, but was inspired by flashes of intuition and philosophical speculation</u>.

In this introductory paragraph, the connection between Harvey and the rise of observation and experiment in the seventeenth century is clear. Moreover, this thesis statement reflects the author's conclusions and anticipates the argument that will follow.

PLAN TO REWRITE YOUR OPENING PARAGRAPH. Because the opening paragraph plays such a crucial role in the overall effectiveness of your paper, you should always plan on revising it several times. In addition, when the paper is complete, it is important to check each section against the introduction. Does each paragraph provide evidence for your thesis? Is it clear to your reader how each point relates to the topic you have established in your introduction? Knowing that you will have to rewrite your introduction in any case can also be reassuring if you are having trouble beginning your paper. Write a rough, temporary opening paragraph, and return to it when you finish your first draft of the entire paper. The act of writing your draft will help you clarify your ideas, your topic, and your argument. It may also help solidify your thesis and your opening.

5a-3. The body

In your introduction, you present your subject and state your thesis. In subsequent paragraphs, you provide evidence for your thesis and answer any objections that could be made to it. The following advice will help you to write well-organized paragraphs and make your argument clear and convincing.

BEGIN EACH PARAGRAPH WITH A TOPIC SENTENCE. Each paragraph should have one driving idea, which is usually asserted in the first sentence, or *topic sentence.* If you have made an outline, your topic sentences will be drawn from the list you made of the main points you wish to cover in your paper. (For advice on making an outline, see 4e.)

MAKE CLEAR CONNECTIONS BETWEEN IDEAS. Each body paragraph provides evidence for your thesis in the form of examples, statistics, and so on. To be convincing, however, your evidence must be clear and well organized. Transitional words and phrases tell your readers how the individual statements in your paragraph are connected. To choose transitions that are appropriate, you will need to consider how your ideas are related to each other. Here are some transitional words or phrases that you might use to indicate particular kinds of relationships:

- **to compare:** *also, similarly, likewise*
- **to contrast:** *on the other hand, although, nevertheless, despite, on the contrary, still, yet, regardless, nonetheless, notwithstanding, whereas, however, in spite of*
- **to add or intensify:** *also, in addition, moreover, furthermore, too, besides, and*

- **to show sequence:** *first* (and any other numerical adjectives), *last, next, finally, subsequently, later, ultimately*
- **to indicate an example:** *for example, for instance, specifically*
- **to indicate cause-and-effect relationships:** *consequently, as a result, because, accordingly, thus, since, therefore, so*

DO NOT WANDER OFF THE SUBJECT. If you include a lot of irrelevant information, you will lose momentum, and your readers will lose the thread of your argument. Be ruthless: Eliminate all extraneous material from the final draft of your paper, however interesting it may be. For instance, if you are writing about the role that Chinese laborers played in the westward expansion of the American railroads, do not spend three paragraphs discussing the construction of the steam locomotive. If your paper concerns the American government's treatment of Japanese citizens during World War II, do not digress into a discussion of naval tactics in the Pacific theater. Similarly, you should avoid repetition and wordy sentences.

WRITING PARAGRAPHS: AN EXAMPLE. Here is a paragraph from the first draft of a paper on Chinese relationships with foreigners during the Ming period:

> **INEFFECTIVE**
>
> The Chinese were willing to trade with barbarians. They distrusted foreigners. Jesuit missionaries were able to establish contacts in China. During the seventeenth century, they acquired the patronage of important officials. They were the emperor's advisers. Chinese women bound their feet, a practice that many Europeans disliked. Relations between China and Europe deteriorated in the eighteenth century. The Jesuits were willing to accommodate themselves to Chinese culture. Chinese culture was of great interest to the scholars of Enlightenment Europe. Matteo Ricci learned about Chinese culture and became fluent in Mandarin. He adopted the robes of a Chinese scholar. He thought that Christianity was compatible with Confucianism. The Jesuit missionaries had scientific knowledge. In the eighteenth century, the papacy forbade Chinese Christians to engage in any form of ancestor worship.

This paragraph is very confusing. In the first place, it has no clear topic sentence; readers have to guess what the writer's main point is. This confusion is compounded by unclear connections between ideas; the paragraph lacks transitional words or phrases that alert readers to the connections that the writer sees between ideas or events. The paragraph is also poorly organized; the writer seems to move at random from topic to topic.

Here is a revised version of the same paragraph:

EFFECTIVE

The Chinese of the Ming dynasty were deeply suspicious of foreigners; *nevertheless*, Jesuit missionaries were able to achieve positions of honor and trust in the imperial court, *ultimately* serving the emperor as scholars and advisers. *At first* glance, this phenomenon seems baffling; upon closer consideration, *however*, it becomes clear that the Jesuits' success was due to their willingness to accommodate themselves to Chinese culture. *For example*, one of the most successful of the early Jesuit missionaries, Matteo Ricci, steeped himself in Chinese culture *and* became fluent in Mandarin. To win the respect of the nobles, he *also* adopted the robes of a Chinese scholar. *Moreover*, he emphasized the similarities between Christianity and Chinese traditions. *Because* of their willingness to adapt to Chinese culture, Jesuit missionaries were accepted by the imperial court until the eighteenth century. Difficulties arose, *however*, when the papacy forbade Chinese Christians to engage in many traditional customs, including any form of ancestor worship. *As a result* of the church's increasing unwillingness to allow such practices, relations between China and Europe deteriorated.

This paragraph has been improved in several ways. First, a topic sentence, (which is underlined) has been added to the beginning. Readers no longer need to guess that this paragraph will address the apparent contrast between sixteenth-century Chinese suspicion of foreigners and the imperial court's acceptance of Jesuit missionaries.

Second, the author has clarified the connections between ideas by including transitional words and phrases. These transitions, (which are italicized) illustrate several different kinds of relationships, including contrast, cause and effect, sequence, and so on, and allow readers to follow the writer's argument.

Third, the paragraph has been reorganized so that the relationships between events are clearer. For example, the revised paragraph states explicitly that relations between

China and European missionaries deteriorated in the eighteenth century because the church became less accommodating to Chinese customs, a relationship obscured in the original paragraph by poor organization.

Finally, the writer has removed references to the practice of foot binding and to European interest in China during the Enlightenment. Both are interesting but irrelevant in a paragraph that deals with Chinese attitudes toward Europeans.

ANTICIPATE AND RESPOND TO COUNTEREVIDENCE AND COUNTERARGUMENTS. Historical issues are seldom clear-cut, and historians often disagree with each other. Effective papers acknowledge disagreement and differing viewpoints. If you discover information that does not support your thesis, do not suppress it. It is important to acknowledge *all* of your data. You should try to explain to your readers why your interpretation is valid, despite the existence of counterevidence, but do not imply that your interpretation is stronger than it is by eliminating data or falsifying your information.

A student writing about the French Revolution, for instance, might argue that the average Parisian worker became a revolutionary not as a result of reading the political arguments of the Enlightenment thinkers but rather from desperate economic need. But the student cannot ignore the fact that many Parisian workers had read such works and that Enlightenment thinkers were often quoted in the popular press. Rather, a successful paper would acknowledge these facts and attempt to show that economic need was a more important or more immediate catalyst for political action.

Remember, too, that it is important to treat opposing viewpoints with respect. It is perfectly legitimate to disagree with the interpretations of other historians. In disagreeing, however, you should never resort to name-calling, oversimplifying, or otherwise distorting opposing points of view. It is important to understand opposing arguments and respond to them fairly.

5a-4. The conclusion

Your paper should not come to an abrupt halt, and yet you do not need to conclude by summarizing everything that you have said in the body of the text. Having read the entire paper, the reader will want to know "So what? Why is this important?" An effective conclusion answers these questions. Thus, it is usually best to end your paper with a paragraph that states the most important conclusions you have reached about your subject and the reasons you think those conclusions are significant.

NOTE: You should avoid introducing new ideas or information in the conclusion. If an idea or fact is important to your argument, you should introduce and discuss it earlier; if it is not, leave it out altogether.

The following is the first draft of the conclusion for the paper on Christian missionaries in China:

INEFFECTIVE

> The Jesuits missionaries were sent to China in the Ming period. Some had good relationships with the emperor, but others didn't. Some learned Mandarin and dressed in court robes. The pope wouldn't let the Chinese worship their ancestors, but some Jesuits thought that Confucianism and Christianity were compatible. Another interesting aspect of Chinese culture at the time was the practice of footbinding.

This conclusion is ineffective for several reasons. First, there are no verbal clues to indicate that this is, in fact, the conclusion. In addition, it is too general and vague; which missionaries had good relationships with the emperor, and which didn't? Moreover, while it lists some of the key elements of the paper, it fails to indicate how these ideas are connected. Most important, perhaps, this conclusion does not suggest why the various ideas presented in the paper are important; it fails, in other words, to answer the questions "So what? Why is this important?" Finally, a new topic is introduced in the last sentence.

In the revised version of the conclusion, these problems have been addressed:

EFFECTIVE

> Thus, it is clear that the success or failure of the Jesuits' missionary activity in China depended largely on the degree to which they were able to adapt to Chinese culture. The most successful missionaries learned Mandarin, adopted Chinese court dress, and looked for parallels between Christianity and the teachings of Confucius. It was only when the Church became more conservative —

> forbidding Chinese Christians, for example, to venerate their ancestors — that the Christian missionary effort in China began to fail. The experience of the Jesuit missionaries in China, then, provides an important clue about what determined the success or failure of missionary activity: ultimately, cultural flexibility may have been a more effective religious ambassador than sophisticated theological arguments.

This conclusion has been improved in several ways. In the first place, it includes key transitional words (*thus, then*) that indicate that the writer is drawing conclusions. It reiterates the important elements of the paper's argument but leaves out information that is either very general ("the Jesuit missionaries were sent to China in the Ming period") or too vague ("some had good relationships with the emperor, but others didn't"). Moreover, unlike the earlier version, it is explicit about how the key topics in the paper — the flexibility of the Jesuit missionaries in adapting to Chinese culture, the parallels the missionaries drew between Christianity and Confucianism, and the institution of more conservative policies — are related. It does not add any new topics, however interesting those topics might be. And, most important, this version, unlike the first draft, clearly outlines the significance of the conclusions that the writer has reached: the Jesuit experience in China tells us something about the relationship between culture and religious belief.

5b. Considering word choice and grammar

It is essential that your writing follow the rules of formal English grammar. Historians are just as concerned as English professors with grammatical issues such as comma placement, subject-verb agreement, sentence fragments, misplaced modifiers, run-on sentences, and unclear antecedents. If you are using a computer, a grammar-check program will help you avoid some of these mistakes, but it is no substitute for learning the rules.

It is beyond the scope of this manual to cover the basic rules of grammar. Any good style guide or writing manual will offer plenty of advice for writing clear grammatical sentences. (See Appendix A for a list of guides.) The following major points are useful to keep in mind when you write in history.

5b-1. Word choice

The words that you choose to express yourself with are a reflection of your own style. Nevertheless, here are a few guidelines.

AVOID CONVERSATIONAL LANGUAGE, SLANG, AND JARGON. Because history papers are usually formal, you should use formal language rather than conversational language and slang. For example, although it is perfectly acceptable in conversational English to say that someone "was a major player" in an event, this expression is too informal for a history paper. In addition, slang often sounds anachronistic: Historians do not usually describe diplomats who fail to negotiate a treaty as having "struck out"; similarly, they describe ideas as archaic or outdated, not "so two minutes ago." Words with double meanings should be used only in their conventional sense: use *sweet* to refer to taste and *radical* to describe something extreme or on the political left. *Awesome* should generally be reserved for awe-inspiring things like Gothic cathedrals. You should also avoid jargon, or specialized language, which can often obscure your meaning.

Finally, contractions (for example, *wasn't* for "was not" or *won't* for "will not") are generally considered too informal for use in a history paper. Rather, you should use the expanded form.

NOTE: Computers have introduced many new words to the English language, but you should avoid misapplying them. For example, until the 1980s, people did not "access" documents or "download" information (and, if you are using books or journals, you are not "accessing" or "downloading" either!). Some other computer jargon to avoid includes the following:

- to interface (for "interact" or "discuss")
- to input (used as a verb, for "add or contribute information")
- databases (for "archives" or "document collections")
- to debug (for "to fix a problem")
- to process (for "to think about carefully" or "understand")

AVOID VALUE-LADEN WORDS. Historians, as noted earlier in this chapter (see 5a-1), attempt to understand the people of the past in their own terms, rather than judge them by the norms of the present. As a result, historians are especially careful to avoid not only anachronisms and generalizations, but also value-laden language in their writing.

It is, of course, tempting to judge past events and people, particularly when they offend our own sense of values. For example, we might criticize the central figures of the American Revolution for their acceptance of slavery as an institution. Labeling these people as "racist" or "hypocritical" does not help us to understand, however, *what* they believed, *why* they believed it, or the social and cultural *context* in which they formed those beliefs. In this case, passing judgment on the people of the past does not help us to understand them or their society.

Other value-laden words that commonly find their way into history papers reflect the writer's sense that his or her own period, culture, and perceptions are superior to those of the past. Examples include: *backward, primitive, uncivilized,* and *superstitious*.

As you write about the past, then, it is important to consider the values that are implied in the words you use to describe your subject, and to choose your words with care.

MAKE YOUR LANGUAGE AS CLEAR AND SIMPLE AS POSSIBLE. In an effort to sound sophisticated, students sometimes use a thesaurus to find a "more impressive" word. The danger of this approach is that the new word might not mean quite what you intended. In general, you should use the simplest word that makes your meaning clear. Do not use a four-syllable word when a single syllable will do. Do not use five words (such as *due to the influence of*) where you can use one (*because*).

AVOID BIASED LANGUAGE. Always take care to avoid words that are gender-biased or that have negative connotations for particular racial, ethnic, or religious groups. You should never use expressions that are clearly derogatory. In addition, you should be aware that many words that were once acceptable are now deemed inappropriate. For example, the use of masculine words or pronouns to refer to both men and women, once a common practice, is now considered sexist by many. Use *humankind* or *people* rather than *mankind,* and do not use a masculine pronoun to refer to people of both genders.

In an attempt to avoid sexist language, students sometimes find themselves making a grammatical error instead. For example, in trying to eliminate the masculine pronoun *his* in the sentence "Each individual reader should form *his* own opinion," a student may write, "Each individual reader should form *their* own opinion." The problem with this new version is that the pronoun *their* is plural, while the antecedent, the word *reader,* is singular. The first version of the sentence is undesirable because it sounds sexist, and the second is unacceptable because it is ungrammatical. A grammatically correct revision is "Individual readers should form their own opinions." In this sentence, the antecedent (*readers*) and the pronoun (*their*) are both plural.

It is also important to realize that you cannot always rely on the books you are reading to alert you to biased language. For example, the author of a fairly recent study of the origins of racism consistently refers to Asian people as "Orientals," a term that was not generally thought derogatory at the time of the book's publication. Since then, however, the word *Oriental* has come to be seen as having a Western bias and should therefore not be used. Another example is the term *Negro,* which once was a respectful term used to refer to people of African descent. Today, the preferred term is *black* or *African American.*

NOTE: You cannot correct the language of your sources. If you are quoting directly, you must use the exact wording of your source, including any racist or sexist language. If you are paraphrasing or summarizing a paragraph containing biased language, you might want to use nonbiased language when it doesn't distort the sense of the source. Otherwise, put biased terms in quotation marks to indicate to your readers that the words are your source's and not yours.

5b-2. Tense

The events that historians write about took place in the past; therefore, historians conventionally use the past tense. Students are sometimes tempted to use the historical present tense for dramatic effect or to make the scene they are describing come alive, as in this example from a student paper:

INEFFECTIVE

The battle rages all around him, but the squire is brave and acquits himself well. He defends his lord fearlessly and

> kills two of the enemy. As the fighting ends, he kneels before his lord on the battlefield, the bodies of the dead and dying all around him. His lord draws his sword and taps it against the squire's shoulders. The squire has proven his worth, and this is his reward; he is now a knight.

This use of the present may be an effective device if you are writing fiction, but it is awkward in a history paper. First, readers might become confused about whether the events under discussion happened in the past or in the present, especially if the paper includes modern assessments of the issue. Second, use of the present makes it easy for the writer to fall prey to anachronism (see 5a-1). Perhaps more important, writing in the present sounds artificial; in normal conversation, we talk about events that happened in the past in the past tense. The same approach is also best for writing.

The present tense *is* used, however, when discussing the contents of documents, artifacts, or works of art because these still exist in the present. Note, for example, the appropriate use of past and present tenses in the following description:

> **EFFECTIVE**
>
> Columbus sailed across an "ocean sea" far greater than he initially imagined. The admiral's *Journal* tells us what Columbus thought he would find: a shorter expanse of water, peppered with hundreds of hospitable islands.

The events of the past are referred to in the past tense (*sailed, imagined, thought*), and the contents of the *Journal* are referred to in the present (*tells*).

5b-3. Voice

In general, historians prefer the active rather than the passive voice. In the *active voice,* the subject of the sentence is also the actor. These two examples both illustrate the active voice:

1. Duke William of Normandy conquered England in 1066.
2. By the seventh century, the Chinese had invented gunpowder, which they used to make fireworks.

In the *passive voice,* the subject of the sentence is not the actor but is acted on. The following sentences transform the previous examples into the passive voice:

1. England was conquered in 1066.
2. The process for making gunpowder was known in the seventh century.

Several difficulties arise when you use the passive voice. Persistent use of the passive voice can make writing sound dull and often makes your writing unnecessarily wordy. More important, however, the passive voice can often obscure meaning and create unnecessary confusion. As you can see from these examples, readers cannot always tell who the actor is. We are not told, for example, who conquered England or who invented gunpowder. Use of the passive voice also allows writers to avoid the complexities of some historical issues. In the second example, for instance, moving from the passive to the active voice forces the writer to be more specific: The Chinese invented gunpowder, but they used it for making fireworks and not for firing weapons.

In addition, using the passive voice in the expressions "it can be argued that" or "it has been argued that" is equivocal. The first expression suggests that the writer is unwilling to take responsibility for his or her arguments. If your evidence leads you to a certain conclusion, state it clearly. Using passive expressions like "it can be argued that" suggests that you are not really sure that your evidence is convincing. Similarly, the expression "it has been argued that" confuses readers: Who has made this argument? How many people and in what context? Readers must have this information to evaluate your argument. Moreover, use of this expression can result in plagiarism. If someone or several persons have argued a particular point, you should identify them in your text itself and in a citation.

This is not to say, however, that you should never use the passive voice. Here, for example, is a description of the Holocaust (verbs in the passive voice have been italicized):

> Hitler engaged in the systematic and ruthless murder of the Jewish people. In 1933, Jews *were forbidden* to hold public office; by 1935, they *were deprived* of citizenship. In all, over six million Jews *were killed* as part of Hitler's "final solution."

In this passage, the writer wants to draw readers' attention to the recipients of the action — the six million Jews killed in the Holocaust. The persons acted on are more important than the actor. The passive voice, which focuses attention on the victims, is therefore appropriate here.

The passive voice, then, can be effective, but it should be used only occasionally and for a specific reason.

5b-4. Use of the pronouns **I, me,** *and* **you**

Although you may occasionally see the pronouns *I, me,* and *you* in history books and journal articles, most professional historians use these pronouns sparingly, or not at all, and most instructors prefer students to avoid them whenever possible. However, a number of professors find their use not only acceptable but actually preferable to more labored constructions like "this evidence leads one to conclude that." Since the conventions governing the use of personal pronouns are in flux, it is best to consult your instructor about his or her preference.

As noted at the beginning of this chapter, the conventions that historians follow in their writing are not a set of rules carved in stone. However, historians read the work of their fellows with certain expectations in mind. They assume that other historians will avoid anachronism and generalizations and respect the subjects of their writing. When they read a history paper, they look for a clearly articulated thesis and the evidence that supports that thesis. And, although they might not articulate these expectations, they follow conventions in their use of tense, voice, and word choice. Understanding and following these conventions will help you produce a paper that more closely conforms to the norms of the profession.

6
Plagiarism: What It Is and How to Avoid It

Plagiarism is the act of taking the words, ideas, or research of another person and putting them forward without citation as if they were your own. It is intellectual theft and a clear violation of the code of ethics and behavior that most academic institutions have established to regulate the scholastic conduct of their members. Most colleges and universities have their own policies that define plagiarism and establish guidelines for dealing with plagiarism cases and punishing offenders, but the penalties for plagiarism are usually severe, ranging from an automatic F in the course to temporary suspension or even permanent expulsion from the school. Plagiarism, in short, is considered a very serious academic offense.

If we look simply at the dictionary definition, it would seem that acts of plagiarism are readily identifiable. And, indeed, some instances of plagiarism *are* obvious; deliberately copying lengthy passages from a book or journal article, or purchasing or downloading whole papers and submitting them as your own work, are clear-cut examples of plagiarism. However, although some students unfortunately make a conscious decision to plagiarize, many more do so inadvertently. This is because, unlike the instances cited above, some situations in which you might use the words or ideas of another may seem murkier. Because of its seriousness, it is essential that you know exactly what kinds of acts constitute plagiarism. This chapter will clarify the concept and give you some advice on how to avoid unintentional plagiarism.

6a. What is plagiarism?

Read the following scenarios. Which of these would be considered plagiarism?

- A student borrows a friend's essay to get some ideas for his own paper. With his friend's permission, he copies portions of it, taking care, however, to cite all the sources his friend included in the original.
- A student finds useful information on a Web site that is not under copyright. She downloads and incorporates sections of this Web site into her paper, but does not cite it since it is in the public domain.
- A student derives some key ideas for his paper from a book. Since he doesn't quote anything directly from this book, he doesn't provide any footnotes. He does, however, include the book in his bibliography.
- A student modifies the original text by changing some words, leaving out an example, and rearranging the order of the material. Since she is not using the exact words of the original, she does not include a footnote.

The answer is that *all four* of these scenarios illustrate examples of plagiarism.

In the first instance, the issue is not whether the student has permission from his friend to use his or her work. As long as the student is submitting work done by another as his own, it is plagiarism. Citing the sources that his friend has used does not mitigate the charge of plagiarism. In the second example, the fact that the student has used material that is not protected by copyright is irrelevant. She is guilty of plagiarism because she has submitted the words of another as her own. The third instance illustrates that the definition of plagiarism encompasses not only the use of someone else's words, but also of their ideas; you must *always* acknowledge the source of your ideas in a footnote or endnote, even if you specifically include the text in your bibliography. Finally, in the fourth example, changing some of the words, reorganizing the material, or leaving out some phrases does not constitute a genuine paraphrase; moreover, even an effective paraphrase requires a footnote.

As a historian, if only for the purposes of one class, you are part of a community of scholars; when you write history papers, you become part of the intellectual conversation of that community. The published words and ideas of other historians are there to be used — but as a matter of intellectual honesty, you are bound to acknowledge their contributions to your own thought.

6b. Avoiding plagiarism

Most unintentional plagiarism can be traced to three sources: confusion about when and how to cite sources, uncertainty about how to paraphrase, and carelessness in taking notes and downloading Internet materials.

6b-1. Citing sources to avoid plagiarism

When you derive facts and ideas from other writers' work, you must cite the sources of your information. Most writers are aware that they must cite the sources of direct quotations. However, students sometimes assume, erroneously, that direct quotations are the *only* things they need to cite. In fact, "borrowing" ideas from other writers without documenting them is a form of plagiarism every bit as serious as taking their words. Therefore, you must provide citations for *all* information derived from another source, even if you have summarized or paraphrased the information. Furthermore, you must also cite your sources when you use other writers' interpretations of a historical event or text. In short, you should remember that any time that you use information derived from another person's work, adopt someone else's interpretation, or build on another writer's ideas, you must acknowledge your source. This enables your readers to distinguish between your ideas and those of others.

The only exception is that you do not need to provide citations for information that is common knowledge. For example, you might have learned from a particular book that the Civil War spanned the years 1861 to 1865, but you do not have to cite the book when you include this fact in your paper. You could have obtained the time span of the Civil War from any number of sources because it is common knowledge. The more you read about your subject, the easier it will be for you to distinguish common knowledge from information that needs a citation. When in doubt, however, it is better to be safe and cite the source. (For additional information on quoting and citing sources, including documentation models, see Chapter 7.)

NOTE: One practice that will help you to avoid plagiarism is to keep all of your research notes and rough drafts in separate files. Then, as you prepare your final draft, you will be able to check your notes if you are uncertain about whether a particular phrase is a direct quote or a paraphrase, or where an idea or quotation came from. (See 4c for more on careful note taking.)

6b-2. Paraphrasing to avoid plagiarism

Most students know that copying a passage word for word from a source is plagiarism. However, many are unsure about how to paraphrase. Consider, for example, this passage from a textbook and the student "paraphrase" that follows:

ORIGINAL PASSAGE

In the early twentieth century, most Latin American nations were characterized by two classes separated by a great gulf. At the top were a small group of European-descended white people, the *patrones* (landlords or patrons), who, along with foreign investors, owned the ranches, mines and plantations of each nation. Like the established families of most societies elsewhere in the world, the *patrones* monopolized the wealth, social prestige, education, and cultural attainments of their nations. Many of them aspired to the ideal of nobility, with high standards of personal morality and a parental concern for those who worked for them. Some *patrones* lived up to these ideals, but most, consciously or unconsciously, exploited their workers.[1]

UNACCEPTABLE PARAPHRASE

In the early part of this century most Latin American countries were typified by two classes separated by a large chasm. At the top were a small group of white people, descended from Europeans, called *patrones*. Along with foreign investors, the *patrones* owned the plantations, ranches, and mines of their countries. Like aristocrats all over the world, the *patrones* controlled the wealth, social status, education, and cultural achievements of their countries. Many of them had high standards of morality and were concerned for their workers, but most, consciously or unconsciously, abused their workers.

1. Richard Goff, Walter Moss, Janice Terry, and Jiu-Hwa Upshur, *The Twentieth Century: A Brief Global History,* 4th ed. (New York: McGraw-Hill, 1994), 62.

In this example, the writer's attempt at paraphrase results in plagiarism, *despite the fact* that the second text is not an exact copy of the original. The writer has used a thesaurus to find synonyms for several words — *characterized* has become *typified, gulf* has been replaced by *chasm,* and *achievements* has been substituted for *attainments*. In addition, several words or phrases in the original have been left out in the second version, and the word order has occasionally been rearranged. Nevertheless, these changes are merely editorial; the new paragraph is not significantly different from the original in either form or substance.

NOTE: This paragraph would be considered plagiarism *even if* the writer acknowledged the source of the material; it is simply too close to the original to be considered the work of the student.

In a genuine paraphrase, the writer has thought about what the source says and absorbed it. Once the writer understands the content of the source, he or she can restate it in an entirely original way that reflects his or her own wording and style. Consider, for example, this paraphrase:

> **ACCEPTABLE PARAPHRASE**
>
> The society of Latin America at the beginning of this century was sharply divided into two groups: the vast majority of the population, made up of the workers, and a wealthy minority, the *patrones,* who were descended from white Europeans. Although the *patrones* represented a very small segment of the population, they controlled the lion's share of their countries' wealth and enjoyed most of the social and educational advantages. Like their counterparts in Europe, many *patrones* adopted an attitude of paternalistic benevolence toward those who worked for them. Even if their concern was genuine, however, the *patrones* clearly reaped the rewards of their workers' labor.[2]

This paraphrase is more successful; the writer has assimilated the content of the source and expressed it in his own words.

NOTE: Even though this is an acceptable paraphrase of the original, and although there are no direct quotations

2. See Richard Goff, Walter Moss, Janice Terry, and Jiu-Hwa Upshur, *The Twentieth Century: A Brief Global History,* 4th ed. (New York: McGraw-Hill, 1994), 62.

used, the author would still need to provide a footnote or endnote indicating the source of this information. You will save time if you paraphrase as you take notes. However, if you attempt to paraphrase with the original source open in front of you, you are courting disaster. To write a genuine paraphrase, you should close the book and rewrite in your own words what you have read. (For advice on taking notes in the form of summaries, see p. 49. A shorter example of paraphrasing can be found on p. 78.)

6b-3. Downloading Internet sources carefully to avoid plagiarism

As with any other source, information derived from the Internet must be properly paraphrased and cited. A particular danger arises, however, from the ease with which Internet material can be downloaded into your working text. Whenever you download material from the Internet, be sure to create a *separate* document file for that material. Otherwise, Internet material may inadvertently become mixed up with your own writing. Moreover, you should keep in mind that Internet sites are more volatile than print sources. Material on many Internet sites is updated on a daily basis, and a site that you find early in your research may be gone by the time you write your final draft. Therefore, you should always record *complete* bibliographic information for each Internet source *as you use it.*

6c. Plagiarism and the Internet

While plagiarism is not a new problem, the opportunities for plagiarism have increased exponentially with the growing popularity of and dependence on the Internet. Careless "cut and paste" note taking poses a real hazard to unwary Internet users. A more distressing and significant problem, however, is the virtual explosion of Web sites offering students the opportunity to buy term papers, or even download them for free. Often presenting themselves as sources of "research assistance," these sites afford countless possibilities for plagiarism under the guise of providing "help" to students who are "in a hurry," "under pressure," or "working on a deadline." Many of these Web sites bury in the "FAQs" (Frequently asked questions) or "About Us" links the caveat that students should use the Web site's papers only as "models" for their own papers. They are, of course, quite right to include this warning. However, before you decide to use the "research assistance" these Web sites claim to provide, consider the criteria for evaluating Internet sites provided in Chapter 2 (see 2b-3).

In determining the usefulness of an Internet site, you should always ask about the author's credentials; for many of these "paper mill" sites, the author of the paper is anonymous and may even be another student. Why, then, should you trust the information the paper provides? Similarly, the Web site's URL should cause you to hesitate; paper mills typically have a ".com" address, rather than the more trustworthy ".edu" or ".gov" suffix that you might expect from a true academic site. You should also consider whether you would really want to list the site in your bibliography; it is not very likely that your professor will be impressed with a bibliographic entry for "schoolisrotten.com."

Finally, if you are ever tempted, you should also realize that if you found the Web site, the chances are good that your professor can find it too. It is not very hard — indeed, it is quite simple — for a professor to track down the source of a plagiarized paper.

NOTE: Ignorance about what constitutes plagiarism is not usually considered an acceptable excuse by college professors, school judicial associations, or university administrators. Read your school's policy on plagiarism and make sure you understand it. Finally, if you have any doubts or need clarification, ask your professors.

7
Quoting and Documenting Sources

Any history paper you write reflects your careful reading and analysis of primary and secondary sources. This section offers general guidance on incorporating source material into your writing through quotation. It also explains the conventions historians use to cite and document sources.

7a. Using quotations

Quotations are an important part of writing in history. Quotations from primary sources provide evidence and support for your thesis. Quotations from secondary sources tell your readers that you are well informed about the current state of research on the issue that you are examining. However, some students go to extremes, producing papers that are little more than a series of quotations loosely strung together. No matter how interesting and accurate the quotations, such a paper is no substitute for your own analysis and discussion of sources. In general, you should minimize your use of quotations, and you should choose the quotations you do use with great care.

The following guidelines will help you to decide when to quote and how to use quotations effectively.

DO NOT QUOTE IF YOU CAN PARAPHRASE. Summarizing or paraphrasing in your own words is usually preferable to direct quotation; it demonstrates that you have digested the information from the source and made it your own.

In particular, you should not quote directly if the quotation would provide only factual information. Examine this passage from *Slave Counterpoint*, a study of eighteenth-century African American culture:

ORIGINAL PASSAGE

Working alongside black women in the fields were boys and girls. Although the age at which a child entered the labor force varied from plantation to plantation, most masters in both Chesapeake and Lowcountry regarded the years of nine or ten as marking this threshold. . . . Black children, unlike their enslaved mothers, do not seem to have been singled out for any more onerous duties than their white counterparts. Those white children who left home to become servants in husbandry in early modern England generally did so at age thirteen to fourteen. However, they had probably been working for neighboring farmers on a nonresident basis from as young as seven.[1]

This passage contains a number of interesting facts. However, while it is clear and well written, there is nothing particularly significant about the wording of the passage *per se;* there are no striking analogies or turns of phrase that are particularly memorable. The paraphrase that follows includes the important facts from the original, but puts them in the writer's own words:

PARAPHRASE

Slave children began to work in the fields with their mothers at around the age of nine or ten. Their experiences as child laborers were similar to those of white children who worked in rural settings in England, where children as young as seven were sent to work on nearby farms, and moved into the homes of their employers in their early teens.

Because the original passage is merely factual, the paraphrase would be preferable to a direct quotation. (For additional information on paraphrasing, see pp. 73–75.)

DO QUOTE IF THE WORDS OF THE ORIGINAL ARE ESPECIALLY MEMORABLE. You might want to quote directly when your source says something in a particularly striking way. In the following passage, Karen Lindsey is describing

1. Philip D. Morgan, *Slave Counterpoint: Black Culture in the Eighteenth-Century Chesapeake and Lowcountry* (Chapel Hill: University of North Carolina Press, 1998), 197.

a key moment in the history of Anne Boleyn, the second wife of King Henry VIII of England. Henry VIII had divorced his first wife, Catherine of Aragon, to marry Anne, who, he hoped, would provide him with a son. By January 1536, Anne had produced a daughter (the future Queen Elizabeth I) and was once again pregnant.

ORIGINAL PASSAGE

On January 29, Catherine of Aragon was buried. On the same day Ann Boleyn, in the chilling phrase of her daughter's biographer, J. E. Neale, "miscarried of her saviour."[2]

The quotation from Neale is memorable because of the imagery he uses to describe Anne's miscarriage, which could not be duplicated in a summary or paraphrase. Lindsey, then, chose an effective quotation.

You might also wish to quote when the original words are important to readers' understanding of the author's intentions or feelings. In the following passage from Plato's *Apology,* Socrates is addressing the jurors who have just condemned him to death:

ORIGINAL PASSAGE

This much I ask from you: [W]hen my sons grow up, avenge yourselves by causing them the same kind of grief that I caused you. . . . Reproach them as I reproach you, that they do not care for the right things and think they are worthy when they are not worthy of anything. If you do this, I shall have been justly treated by you, and my sons also.[3]

In this passage, the tone is as important as the content. It would be impossible to capture in a summary or paraphrase the irony of the original.

7a-1. Conventions for using quotations

When you quote, you must follow the conventions for using quotation marks and integrating quotations in the text of your paper. Keep in mind the following important points.

2. Karen Lindsey, *Divorced, Beheaded, Survived: A Feminist Reinterpretation of the Wives of Henry VIII* (Reading, Mass.: Perseus Books, 1995), 115.

3. Plato, *Apology,* in *Five Dialogues,* trans. G. M. A. Grube (Indianapolis: Hackett, 1981), 44.

INDICATE WHERE YOUR QUOTATION BEGINS AND ENDS. If you quote a source, you should quote the source's words *exactly,* and you should enclose the material from your source in quotation marks. If your quotation is more than four typed lines, you should set the quotation off by indenting it; this is called a *block quotation.* (The quotation from Socrates is an example of a block quotation.) Block quotations are *not* enclosed in quotation marks. Typically, long quotations are preceded by an introductory sentence followed by a colon. You should use block quotations sparingly, if at all. Frequent use of long quotations suggests that you have not really understood the material well enough to paraphrase (see p. 74). Moreover, a long quotation can be distracting and cause readers to lose the thread of your argument. You should therefore use a lengthy quotation only if you have a compelling reason to do so.

KEEP QUOTATIONS BRIEF. To keep quoted material to a minimum, you should condense quoted passages by using the ellipsis mark (three periods, with spaces between), which indicates that you have left out some of the original material. If you are leaving out material at the end of a sentence, the ellipsis should be followed by a period (i.e., there will be *four* periods). The preceding quotation from Plato's *Apology* contains an example of this method.

FRAME YOUR QUOTATION. Quotations from sources cannot simply be dropped into your paper. Even if a quotation is appropriate to a point you are making, you cannot assume that its significance is immediately obvious to your readers. You should always make it clear to your readers how the quotation you have chosen supports your argument. This example is from a student paper on Judge Benjamin Lindsey, the founder of the first juvenile court in the United States:

> Like most progressives, Lindsey was interested in social reform. "I found no 'problem of the children' that was not also the problem of their parents."[4]

It is not clear how the quotation illustrates the writer's statement that Lindsey was interested in social reform. Are readers meant to assume that Lindsey wanted to

4. Benjamin Barr Lindsey, *The Beast* (New York: Doubleday, 1910), 151.

remove children from the homes of unfit parents? Provide government support for indigent parents? Encourage state-funded family counseling?

In the revised version, the student frames the quotation in a way that makes its significance clear:

> Noting that youthful offenders were often the product of criminal environments, Lindsey argued that even the most vigorous attempts to curb juvenile delinquency would fail until more sweeping social reforms eliminated the economic and social factors that led their parents to engage in illegal activities. Addressing the need to rehabilitate and reeducate adult criminals, he wrote: "I found no 'problem of the children' that was not also the problem of their parents." Thus, for Lindsey, the reform of the juvenile justice system was intrinsically linked to the reform of adult criminal courts.

In this revision, the significance of the quotation as it pertains to the writer's argument is clear. The writer's analysis before and after the quotation puts Lindsey's words in context.

7b. Documenting sources

For all of the sources in your paper, including visual and other nonwritten materials, you must provide complete bibliographic information. This is important for two reasons. First, it gives appropriate credit to your sources. In addition, bibliographic information enables readers to look up your sources to evaluate your interpretation of them or to read more extensively from them.

7b-1. Footnotes and endnotes

Historians typically use footnotes or endnotes to document their sources. With this method, you place a raised number, called a *superscript,* at the end of the last word of a quotation, paraphrase, or summary. This number corresponds to a numbered note that provides bibliographic information about your source. Notes may be placed at the bottom of the page (footnotes) or at the end of the paper (endnotes). In either case, notes should be numbered consecutively from the beginning to the end of the paper.

The following example shows a source cited in the text of a paper and documented in a footnote or endnote:

TEXT

Spurlock notes that when mesmerism came to America in 1836, "it was a method of curing sickness — a scientific triumph over magic."[5]

NOTE

5. John C. Spurlock, *Free Love: Marriage and Middle-Class Radicalism in America,* 1825–1860 (New York: New York University Press, 1988), 85.

You should ask your instructor if he or she has a preference for footnotes or endnotes. If the choice is left up to you, weigh the advantages and disadvantages of each form. Footnotes allow your readers to refer easily and quickly to the sources cited on a given page, but they can be distracting. Further, historians often use explanatory or discursive notes, which contain more than simple bibliographic information. (For an example of a discursive footnote, see footnote 3 from the sample paragraph on page 84.) If your paper has a large number of such footnotes in addition to bibliographic footnotes, the pages might look overwhelmed with notes. If you use endnotes, you do not need to worry about the length of your notes. However, endnotes are less accessible, requiring readers to turn to the end of the paper to refer to each note.

7b-2. Bibliography

Papers with footnotes or endnotes also need to have a bibliography — a list of all the sources cited in the paper, arranged alphabetically by authors' last names (or by title where there is no author). In a paper with endnotes, the bibliography always follows the last endnote page. (See p. 118 for a sample bibliography.)

NOTE: An alternative form of documentation that is commonly used in professional journals in the social sciences is the author-date system. The author's last name and the publication date of a cited source are included in parentheses in the text itself; complete bibliographic information appears in a reference list at the end of the text. This form of documentation is almost never used in history because the author-date system is generally not practical for documenting many of the primary sources historians use. Occasionally, a history professor may suggest the use of the author-date system for a book review or for a paper citing only one or two sources, but you should not use it unless you are specifically told to do so.

7b-3. Documenting Internet sources

The Internet is an increasingly important tool for historical research. Since it is still a relatively new tool, however, the conventions for documenting online sources are not yet firmly established. Nevertheless, it is essential that you provide your reader with enough information to locate and examine the material you have obtained from the Internet.

One useful source of information for documenting electronic sources is *Online! A Reference Guide to Using Internet Sources* by Andrew Harnack and Eugene Kleppinger (Boston: Bedford/St. Martin's, 2000). Documentation models for Internet and other electronic sources can also be found in this manual on pages 98–102 and 112–114.

7b-4. Documenting nonwritten materials

Maps, graphs, photographs, cartoons, and other nonwritten materials can be useful in a history paper. It is not enough, however, to add these materials to your paper without discussion or explanation. When they appear in the body of a paper, visual materials, like quotations, should be incorporated into the text. Each image should include a caption that identifies it, and the text accompanying any visual material should explain its significance and its relationship to the topic of discussion. If you group visual materials in an appendix to your paper, you will also need to supply captions that identify the materials and their sources. Of course, using maps, photographs, and other nonwritten materials without full citations constitutes plagiarism. Like any other source, nonwritten materials must be cited in the bibliography.

7c. Using quotations and documenting sources: An example

A well-written history paper incorporates and documents source material. In the following paragraph, the writer has further revised the paragraph shown on pages 62–63 to include short quotations, block quotations, citations of both primary and secondary sources, and a discursive footnote:

The Chinese of the Ming dynasty were generally "uninterested in, and at times hostile to, things foreign."[1] The comments of one Ming official, Chang Han, reflect the attitude of many of his contemporaries:

> Foreigners are recalcitrant and their greed knows no bounds. . . . What is more, the greedy heart is unpredictable. If one day they break the treaties and invade our frontiers, who will be able to defend us against them?[2]

Despite this distrust, Jesuit missionaries were able to achieve positions of honor and trust in the imperial court, ultimately serving the emperor as scholars and advisers. It seems clear that the Jesuits' success in establishing cordial relations with the Chinese court was due to their initial willingness to accommodate themselves to Chinese culture. For example, realizing the extent to which the Chinese distrusted foreigners, one of the most successful of the early Jesuit missionaries, Matteo Ricci, steeped himself in Chinese culture and became fluent in Mandarin. Recognizing the importance of converting the highly educated members of the court,[3] Ricci adopted the robes of a Chinese scholar.[4] Moreover, he emphasized the similarities between Christianity and Chinese tradition, presenting Christianity as "a system of wisdom and ethics compatible with Confucianism."[5] Because of their willingness to adapt to Chinese culture, Jesuit missionaries were accepted by the imperial court until the eighteenth century. Difficulties arose, however, when the papacy forbade Chinese Christians to engage in many traditional customs, including any form of ancestor worship.[6] As the church became less accommodating to Chinese culture, relations between China and Europe deteriorated.

1. John K. Fairbank and Edwin O. Reischauer, *China: Tradition and Transformation,* rev. ed. (Boston: Houghton Mifflin, 1989), 179.

2. Chang Han, "Essay on Merchants," trans. Lily Hwa, in *Chinese Civilization and Society: A Sourcebook,* ed. Patricia Buckley Ebrey (New York: Free Press, 1981), 157.

3. The conversion of highly placed and influential officials, whose decisions might lead to conversions not only within their own households but within court circles, was an important goal for many early missionaries. For a discussion of important converts to Christianity among educated Chinese, see Jacques Gernet, *A History of Chinese Civilization,* trans. J. R. Foster and Charles Hartman, 2d ed. (Cambridge: Cambridge University Press, 1996), 456–58.

4. Gernet, 450.

5. Fairbank and Reischauer, 245.

6. Gernet, 519; Fairbank and Reischauer, 249.

7d. Documentation models

The following models of notes and bibliographic entries illustrate the types of sources commonly used in history. The models follow *The Chicago Manual of Style,* 14th ed. (Chicago: University of Chicago Press, 1993), which is the documentation format usually preferred by historians. Your professor will probably tell you which style guide to use. (Many instructors ask their students to use Kate L. Turabian's *A Manual for Writers,* which follows *The Chicago Manual.*) Whatever style you use, be consistent: If your first footnote or endnote follows the *Chicago Manual* form, all of your notes and your bibliography should follow the *Chicago Manual.*

NOTE: Notes and bibliographies follow different forms. The following example, which models a note and a bibliography entry for the same book, illustrates the differences in these two forms.

NOTE

1. Elizabeth A. Fenn, *Pox Americana: The Great Smallpox Epidemic of 1775–82* (New York: Hill and Wang, 2001), 115.

BIBLIOGRAPHY

Fenn, Elizabeth A. *Pox Americana: The Great Smallpox Epidemic of 1775–82.* New York: Hill and Wang, 2001.

As you compare these two models, you will notice several differences:

- The note begins with an indentation and is numbered, while the first line of the bibliographic entry begins at the far left, and subsequent lines are indented.
- In the note form, the author's name appears in the conventional order (first name, middle initial, last name), while the bibliography lists authors by their last names; the first name and initials are separated from the last name by a comma.
- Commas separate the author and title in the note, while the author's name and the title are followed by periods in the bibliography.
- In the note form, the place of publication, the publisher, and the date are enclosed in parentheses; in the bibliography, no parentheses are used.
- The note refers the reader to the specific pages being cited; the bibliography cites the book.

Documentation Models for Footnotes and Endnotes

Source

Models for notes are given on pages 86 to 102. Bibliographic entries for the same sources are given on pages 102 to 114 and are distinguished by the darker side band.

7d-1. Models for footnotes and endnotes

Books

A typical note for a book includes the following information:

- The author's full name (or the editor's full name, if no author is listed), followed by a comma;
- The full title of the book, italicized or underlined;
- Publication information: the city of publication, followed by a colon (no state is needed for well-known cities); the name of the publisher, followed by a comma ("Inc.," "Co.," and other abbreviations are not needed); and the date of publication — all enclosed in parentheses and followed by a comma;
- The page or pages cited, followed by a period.

Individual entries should be single-spaced; double-space between notes. Typically, the first line of each note is indented.

BASIC FORM FOR A BOOK

1. Jonathan Waterman, *Arctic Crossing: A Journey through the Northwest Passage and Innuit Culture* (New York: Alfred A. Knopf, 2001), 167.

SHORTENED FORMS IN SUBSEQUENT REFERENCES

The first time you cite a work, you must provide complete bibliographic information. In subsequent references, however, use a shortened form. There are two acceptable methods to shorten a reference. In one, you can cite the author's last name followed by a comma and the page or pages cited.

2. Waterman, 290.

In the second, you may also include a shortened form of the title in your subsequent reference. This is necessary if you cite more than one work by the same author in your paper or if a subsequent reference appears long after the first reference. To shorten the title, use the key word or words from the title of the book or article.

3. Waterman, *Arctic Crossing,* 301.

ABBREVIATIONS IN SUBSEQUENT REFERENCES

Ibid. The abbreviation "ibid." (from the Latin *ibidem,* meaning "in the same place") is sometimes used to refer to the work cited in the previous note. However, many professors and professional journals prefer the author/page or the author/short title/page style. Be sure you know which method your professor prefers.

When it is used, "ibid." stands in place of both the author's name and the title of the work. If you are referring to the same page, use "ibid." alone; if you are referring to different page numbers, use "ibid." followed by a comma and the new page numbers.

4. Ibid., 79–84.

NOTE: Never use "ibid." if the previous note refers to more than one work.

Idem If you are citing several works by the same author within the same note, you can use the word "idem" (Latin for "the same") in place of the author's name after the first reference.

5. Samuel Brunk, *Revolution and Betrayal: A Life of Emiliano Zapata* (Albuquerque: University of New Mexico Press, 1995), 288; idem, "The Sad Situation of Civilians and Soldiers: The Banditry of Zapatismo in the Mexican Revolution," *American Historical Review* 101 (1996): 342.

Op. cit. and *loc. cit.* The *Chicago Manual* discourages the use of either "op. cit." (meaning "in the work cited") or "loc. cit." ("in the place cited") to refer to the title of a work cited earlier. Use one of the two shortened forms instead.

TWO OR MORE AUTHORS

If a book has two or more authors, list the authors in your note in the order in which their names appear on the title page.

6. James Bradley and Ron Powers, *Flags of Our Fathers* (New York: Bantam Books, 2000), 78–80.

NOTE: For books with more than three authors, you may use the Latin term "et al." ("and others") after the first author instead of listing all the authors (for example, "Jane Doe et al.").

AUTHOR'S NAME IN THE TITLE

Sometimes an author's name appears in the title of a book, as in an autobiography or a collection of letters or papers. In this case, your footnote or endnote should begin with the title of the book.

7. *Charles Darwin's Letters: A Selection, 1825–1859,* ed. Frederick Burkhardt (Cambridge: Cambridge University Press, 1996), 15–19.

ANONYMOUS WORK

If the author of a work is unknown and if there is no editor or compiler, begin your note with the title.

8. *DK Atlas of World History* (New York: Dorling Kindersley, 2000), 33.

EDITED OR COMPILED WORK WITHOUT AN AUTHOR

Cite a book by its editor (abbreviated "ed.") or compiler (abbreviated "comp.") if no author appears on the title page (as in a collection or anthology).

9. Gregory L. Freeze, ed., *Russia: A History* (New York: Oxford University Press, 2000), 65–66.

EDITED WORK WITH AN AUTHOR

If an author's name is provided in addition to an editor's, give the editor's name after the title.

10. Efraim Karsh, *Empires of the Sand: The Struggle for Mastery in the Middle East, 1789–1923,* ed. Inari Karsh (Cambridge: Harvard University Press, 1999), 303–04.

A book with multiple editors should be treated the same way as a book with multiple authors; list the editors in the order in which they appear on the title page.

11. Robert M. Levine and John L. Crocitti, eds., *The Brazil Reader: History, Culture, Politics* (Durham, N.C.: Duke University Press, 1999), 436.

TRANSLATED WORK

A translator's name, like an editor's, is placed after the title when an author's name is given. If a source has an editor and a translator, then both should be listed.

12. Xie Bingying, *A Woman Soldier's Own Story,* trans. Barry Brissman and Lily Chia Brissman (New York: Columbia University Press, 2001), 296.

13. Roman Vishniac, *Children of a Vanished World,* S. Mark Taper Foundation Book in Jewish Studies, ed. Mara Vishniac Kohn, trans. Miriam Hartman Flacks (Berkeley: University of California Press, 1999), 23.

MULTIVOLUME WORK

You can cite material from a single volume in a multivolume work in one of two ways. You can give the name of the volume first:

14. *The Wartime Genesis of Free Labor: The Upper South,* ed. Ira Berlin, vol. 1 of *Freedom: A Documentary History of Emancipation, 1861–1867* (New York: Cambridge University Press, 1993), 321–23.

or you can give the series name first:

15. *Freedom: A Documentary History of Emancipation,* 1861–1867, vol. 1, *The Wartime Genesis of Free Labor: The Upper South,* ed. Ira Berlin (New York: Cambridge University Press, 1993), 321–23.

If an individual volume of a multivolume work does not have its own title, include the volume number and the page numbers after the publication information.

16. *Cambridge History of American Foreign Relations* (Cambridge: Cambridge University Press, 1993), 1:32–33.

ARTICLE OR DOCUMENT IN A COLLECTION OR ANTHOLOGY

If you cite an article or document in a collection or anthology, include the author and title of the article, followed by the title, editor, and publication information for the book in which it appears. Also give the page or pages on which the information you are citing appears.

17. Thomas H. Huxley, "The Darwinian Hypothesis," in *Galileo's Commandment: An Anthology of Great Science Writing,* ed. Edmund Blair Bolles (New York: W. H. Freeman, 1997), 259.

CHAPTER IN AN EDITED WORK

When you are citing a book that has an editor or multiple editors, but in which the chapters have individual authors, you should cite the author and title of the chapter first, followed by the title, editor, and publication information for the book.

18. Harold E. L. Prins, "Children of Gluskap: Wabanaki Indians on the Eve of the European Invasion," in *American Beginnings: Exploration, Culture, and Cartography in the Land of Norumbega,* ed. Emerson W. Baker et al. (Lincoln and London: University of Nebraska Press, 1994), 98–99.

LETTER IN A PUBLISHED COLLECTION

When citing a letter that appears in a published collection, list the sender, recipient, and date of the communication, and then cite the collection as you would a book.

19. An Expectant Mother to Eleanor Roosevelt, 2 January 1935, *America 1900–1999: Letters of the Century,* ed. Lisa Grunwald and Stephen J. Adler (New York: Dial Press, 1999), 223.

EDITION OTHER THAN THE FIRST

If the text you are using is not the first edition, provide the edition number in your note.

20. Chafe, William H., *The Unfinished Journey: America since World War II,* 5th ed. (New York: Oxford University Press, 2002), 247.

WORK IN A SERIES

Some books are part of a series: publications on the same general subject that are supervised by a general editor or group of editors. The series title and series editor may be eliminated from your note if the book can be located easily without them.

21. Robert H. Abzug, *America Views the Holocaust, 1933–1945,* Bedford Series in History and Culture, ed. Natalie Zemon Davis and Ernest R. May (Boston: Bedford/St. Martin's, 1999), 194–197.

Periodicals

A typical note for an article in a journal includes the following information:

- The author's full name, followed by a comma;
- The title of the article, in quotation marks and followed by a comma;
- The name of the journal in which the article appears, italicized or underlined;
- The volume number (in arabic numerals, even if the journal uses roman numerals);
- The date, in parentheses, followed by a colon;
- The page or pages cited, followed by a period.

ARTICLE IN A JOURNAL PAGINATED BY VOLUME

Most scholarly journals are paginated consecutively throughout the volume. When citing an article from such a journal, you do not need to give the issue number, although this information may be useful, especially for recent, unbound journals.

22. Ned C. Landsman, "Nation, Migration, and the Province in the First British Empire: Scotland and the Americas, 1600–1800," *American Historical Review* 104 (1999): 463.

ARTICLE IN A JOURNAL PAGINATED BY ISSUE

If a journal paginates each issue separately, you must provide the issue number. In the following model (one of several acceptable forms for citing the issue of a journal), the volume number is 283, the issue number is 5, the year of publication is 2000, and the page reference is 668.

23. Rhoda Wynn, "Saints and Sinners: Women and the Practice of Medicine throughout the Ages," *Journal of the American Medical Association* 283, no. 5 (2000): 668.

NOTE: If you wish to include the month of publication, put it before the year: (March 2000). If you include the month, you do not need the issue number.

ARTICLE IN A POPULAR MAGAZINE

In citing an article from a popular magazine, include the author, title of the article, magazine title, and date (not in parentheses). Omit the volume and issue numbers. It is not necessary to include page numbers; if you do include them, they should be preceded by a comma, not a colon.

24. Evan Thomas, "The Day That Changed America," *Newsweek Special Double Issue,* December 2001–January 2002, 45–46.

NEWSPAPER ARTICLE

When referring to an article in a daily newspaper, always cite the author's name (if it is given), the title of the article, date, month, and year. Each issue of a newspaper may go through several editions, and in each edition articles may be rearranged or even eliminated entirely. For this reason, you should cite the name of the edition in which the article appeared (for example, first edition, late edition). Page numbers are usually omitted. If you are citing a large newspaper that is published in sections, include the name, letter, or number of the section.

25. Dean E. Murphy, "A Single Grief Knits Together a Vast Country," *New York Times,* 12 September 2002, sec. A, late edition.

NOTE: If the city of the newspaper is not well known, include the state in parentheses.

BOOK REVIEW

To cite a book review, begin with the reviewer's name followed by the title of the review, if one is given. Follow this information by the words "review of," the title of the work being reviewed, and its author. Also cite the periodical in which the review appears and the relevant publication information. If the author of the review is not named, begin with the title of the review or, if the review is untitled, with the words "Review of."

26. Ilene Cooper, review of *Nat Turner's Slave Rebellion in American History,* by Judith Edwards, *Booklist* 96 (2000): 1093.

27. Review of *A Middle East Mosaic: Fragments of Life, Letters and History,* by Bernard Lewis, ed., *Publishers Weekly,* 24 March 2000, 80.

Public documents

In the United States, most federal government publications are printed by the Government Printing Office in Washington, D.C., and may be issued by both houses of Congress (the House of Representatives and the Senate); by the executive departments (for example, the Department of State, the Department of the Interior, and so on); or by government commissions or agencies (for example, the Securities and Exchange Commission). In addition, public documents may be issued by state or local governments. A reference to a public document should include the following:

- The name of the country, state, city, or county from which the document was issued (papers on United States history may omit "United States" or "U.S.");
- The name of the legislative body, court, executive department, or other agency issuing the document;
- The title of the document or collection, if given;
- The name of the author, editor, or compiler;
- The report number;
- The publisher, if applicable ("Government Printing Office" may be shortened to "GPO");
- The date;
- The page or pages cited.

The following models are for notes citing government documents commonly used by students writing history papers.

PRESIDENTIAL PAPERS

The Government Printing Office has published the papers of the presidents of the United States in two multivolume collections: *Compilation of the Messages and Papers of the Presidents, 1789–1897* for the early presidency and *Public Papers of the Presidents of the United States* for twentieth-century presidents.

28. Dwight D. Eisenhower, *Public Papers of the Presidents of the United States: Dwight D. Eisenhower,* 1953 (Washington, D.C.: GPO, 1960), 228–30.

EXECUTIVE DEPARTMENT DOCUMENT

A note for a document issued by one of the executive departments begins with the issuing department. Include the name of the author of the document, if it is known. If the publication is part of a series, you may include the series number and omit the publication information.

29. U.S. General Accounting Office, *Desert Shield and Desert Storm Reports and Testimonies,* 1991–93 (Washington, D.C.: General Accounting Office, 1994), 446.

30. U.S. Department of State, *Belarus,* Background Notes Series, no. 10344, 77.

TESTIMONY BEFORE A COMMITTEE

Transcripts of testimony presented before congressional committees or commissions can be found in records called "hearings." Begin the note with the committee or commission name.

31. Senate Committee on Foreign Relations, *Countering the Changing Threat of International Terrorism: Report of the National Commission on Terrorism: Hearing before the Committee on Foreign Relations,* 106th Cong., 2nd sess., 2000, 53.

CONGRESSIONAL COMMITTEE PRINT

Both houses of Congress issue research reports called "Committee Prints." Your note should include either the date or the Committee Print number, if one is provided.

32. U.S. Congress, House Committee on International Relations, *International Terrorism: A Compilation of Major Laws, Treaties, Agreements, and Executive Documents,* 106th Cong., 2nd sess., 2000, Committee Print, 229–31.

TREATY

Treaties can be found in volumes of *United States Treaties and Other International Agreements,* issued by the Government Printing Office. Each treaty in the bound volume was originally published in pamphlet form in a State Department series titled Treaties and Other International Acts (TIAS). In your note, the title (in quotation marks) and date of a treaty should follow the name of the issuing agency (such as U.S. Department of State). The number assigned to the treaty in TIAS is given in the bound volume and should also be included in your note.

33. U.S. Department of State, "Jay Treaty," 19 November 1794, TIAS no. 105, *United States Treaties and Other International Agreements,* vol. 2, 245.

UNITED STATES CONSTITUTION

The Constitution is cited by article (abbreviated "art.") or amendment ("amend.") and section ("sec.").

34. U.S. Constitution, art. 4, sec. 1.

The forms of notes for state and local government publications are the same as those for federal government publications.

Other sources

UNPUBLISHED THESIS OR DISSERTATION

To cite an unpublished thesis or dissertation, give its author, title (in quotation marks), academic institution, and date.

35. Robert James Nemes, "Between Reform and Revolution: Associations, Culture, and Politics in Budapest, 1800–1849" (Ph.D. diss., Columbia University, 1999), 170.

UNPUBLISHED LETTER IN A MANUSCRIPT COLLECTION

When citing material from manuscript collections, begin with the specific item, followed by its location. For a letter, start with the name of the letter writer, followed by the name of the recipient and the date. Full identifying information about the collection in which the letter is found should follow, beginning with the file, box or container number, if known; the name of the collection; and its location.

36. Nathaniel Hawthorne to James W. Beekman, 9 April 1853, letter box 3, "James W. Beekman Papers," New-York Historical Society, New York.

ILLUSTRATION OR MAP

In citing an illustration or map in a printed text, give both the page number on which the illustration or map appears and the figure or plate number, if one is provided.

37. Time/CBS News, *People of the Century* (New York: Simon & Schuster, 1999), 159.

38. Walter D. Mignolo, *The Darker Side of the Renaissance: Literacy, Territoriality, and Colonization* (Ann Arbor: University of Michigan Press, 1995), 273, Fig. 6.11.

SOUND RECORDING

Notes for sound recordings, including audiotapes, compact discs, and records, begin with the composer's name followed by the title of the recording (italicized or underlined) and the name of the performer. Also provide the name of the recording company and the number.

39. Gustav Holst, *The Planets,* Royal Philharmonic Orchestra, André Previn, Telarc compact disc 80133.

For an anonymous work or a collection of works by several composers, begin with the title.

40. *Virtuoso Recorder Music,* Amsterdam Loeki Stardust Quartet, Decca compact disc 414 277-2.

FILM, VIDEOCASSETTE, OR DVD

A note for a film, videocassette, or DVD should include the title of the episode (if part of a series), the title of the film, the name of the producer and director, the playing time, the name of the production company, and the date. Videocassettes and DVD's should be identified as such.

41. "Forever Free," *The Civil War,* prod. Ken Burns, 11 hours, PBS Video, 1990, videocassette.

INTERVIEW

A note for an interview that has been published or broadcast on radio or television should include the name of the person interviewed, the title of the interview (if any), the name of the person who conducted the interview, the medium in which the interview appeared (radio, television, book, journal), and the facts of publication.

42. Timothy McVeigh, interviewed by Ed Bradley, *60 Minutes,* Columbia Broadcasting System, 26 March 2000.

PERSONAL COMMUNICATION

A note for an interview you have conducted in person or by telephone should include the name of the person you interviewed, the words "interview by author," the place of the interview, if applicable, and the date of the interview.

43. Nico Milkov, telephone interview by author, 2 October 2002.

A personal letter or memorandum to you should be cited in the same way as a personal interview.

44. Audrey Hamilton, letter to author, 15 March 2003.

REFERENCE WORK

In a note for a standard reference work that is arranged alphabetically, such as a dictionary or an encyclopedia, omit the publication information, as well as the volume and page references. You must, however, note the edition if it is not the first. After the name and edition of the work, use the abbreviation "s.v." (for *sub verbo,* "under the word") followed by the title of the entry in quotation marks.

45. *Encyclopaedia Britannica,* 15th ed., s.v. "steam power."

46. *Merriam-Webster's Collegiate Dictionary,* 10th ed., s.v. "civilization."

BIBLICAL REFERENCE

When referring to a passage from the Bible, cite the book (abbreviated), chapter, and verse, either in the text or in a note. Do not provide a page number. In your first biblical reference, identify the version of the Bible you are using; in subsequent references, abbreviate the version.

47. Matt. 20.4–9 Revised Standard Version.

48. 1 Chron. 4.13–15 RSV.

Chapters and verses in biblical references have traditionally been separated by a colon, but in current usage they are separated by a period.

INDIRECT SOURCE

If material you wish to use from a source has been taken from another source, it is always preferable to find and consult the original source. If this is not possible, you must acknowledge both the original source of the material and your own source for the information.

49. George Harmon Knoles, *The Jazz Age Revisited: British Criticism of American Civilization during the 1920s* (Stanford: Stanford University Press, 1955), 31, quoted in C. Vann Woodward, *The Old World's New World* (Oxford: Oxford University Press, 1991), 46.

Electronic sources

The most recent edition of *The Chicago Manual of Style* does not include guidelines for Internet citations. However, one model that the University of Chicago Press recommends is the citation method found in *Online! A Reference Guide to Using Internet Sources* by Andrew Harnack and Eugene Kleppinger (Boston: Bedford/St. Martin's, 2000). An online version is available at <bedfordstmartins .com/online>.

To cite a document that is available on the World Wide Web, the following information should be included: the author's name, if known; the title of the document, in quotation marks; the title of the complete work, if applicable, in italics or underlined; the date of the publication or last revision (if not known, use "n.d."); the URL (uniform resource locator), in angle brackets; and the date of access, in parentheses.

WHOLE WEB SITE WITH A KNOWN AUTHOR

If you wish to cite a complete Web site, include the author's name; the title of the Web site italicized or underlined; the date that the site was posted or most recently revised (if known); the URL, in angle brackets; and the date on which the site was accessed, in parentheses.

50. Jon Elliston, *The Bay of Pigs Invasion,* 1996, <www.parascope.com/articles/1296/bayofpigs.htm> (5 August 2002).

WHOLE WEB SITE WITH AN UNKNOWN AUTHOR

If you are citing a Web site whose authorship is unknown, begin with the title of the Web site.

51. *Military History On-Line,* 2000, <www.militaryhistoryonline.com/> (4 July 2000).

SELECTION FROM A WEB SITE

To cite a selection from a Web site, list the author (if known); the title of the selection, in quotation marks; the title of the complete work, italicized or underlined; the date of publication or last revision (if known); the URL, in angle brackets; and the date on which the site was accessed, in parentheses.

52. Douglas Linder, "An Account of Events in Salem," *Famous Trials,* June 2001, <www.law.umkc.edu/faculty/projects/ftrials/salem/sal_acct.htm> (23 September 2002).

ONLINE BOOK

A citation for an online book should include the following information: the author of the book; the title of the book, italicized or underlined; the place and date of publication (if known), in parentheses; the project title and date; the URL, in angle brackets; and the date on which the site was accessed, in parentheses.

53. Alfred Russell Wallace, *The Malay Archipelago* (1869), Project Gutenberg, February 2001, <ftp://ibiblio.org/pub/docs/books/gutenberg/etext01/1malay10.txt> (6 January 2003).

If you have accessed an online book through an authored Web site, your note should also include the author, name, and date of the Web site, if known.

54. Cotton Mather, *Memorable Providences, Relating to Witchcrafts and Possessions* (Boston: 1689), at Douglas Linder, *Famous Trials,* 2002, <www.law.umkc.edu/faculty/projects/ftrials/salem/asa_math.htm> (22 October 2002).

ARTICLE IN AN ELECTRONIC JOURNAL

A citation for an article in an electronic journal should include the author's name; the title of the article, in quotation marks; the title of the journal, italicized or underlined; the number of the journal; the date of publication, in parentheses; the URL, in angle brackets; and the date of access, in parentheses.

55. Arthur Lindly, "The Ahistoricism of Medieval Film," *Screening the Past* 3 (1998), <www.latrobe.edu.au/screeningthepast/firstrelease/fir598/ALfr3a.htm> (15 May 2001).

ARTICLE ACCESSED THROUGH AN ELECTRONIC DATABASE

To cite an article from a print journal accessed through an electronic database, add the following to the information you would include for a journal article in print: the name of the online database; the URL for the database, in angle brackets; and the date of access, in parentheses.

56. Robert Brent Toplin, "The Filmmaker as Historian," *American Historical Review* 93 (1988): 1210–27, online via JSTOR, <www.jstor.org/> (2 November 1999).

ONLINE GOVERNMENT PUBLICATION

A citation for a government publication should include the author; the title of the document; the type of document; the date of publication; the URL, in angle brackets; and the date of access, in parentheses.

57. George W. Bush, "Creation of the President's Council on Bioethics," Executive Order, 28 November 2001, <www.whitehouse.gov/news/releases/2001/11/20011128_13.html> (17 October 2002).

ONLINE NEWSPAPER ARTICLE

To cite an online newspaper article, include the author, if known; the title of the article; the name of the newspaper; the date of publication; the URL, in angle brackets; and the date of access, in parentheses.

58. Ellen Nakashima and Alan Sipress, "Bali Bombing Suspect Linked to Allies of Al Qaeda," *WashingtonPost.com,* 11 November 2002, <www.washingtonpost.com/wp_dyn/articles/A37002_2002Nov10.html> (29 December 2002).

ONLINE REVIEW

A citation for an online review should include the name of the reviewer; the title and author of the book being reviewed; the name of the online publication; the date of the review; the URL, in angle brackets; and the date of access, in parentheses.

59. Serge Schmemann, review of *Natasha's Dance,* by Orlando Figes, *New York Times on the Web,* 10 November 2002, <www.nytimes.com/2002/11/10/books/review/10schmemt.html> (16 January 2003).

WEB DISCUSSION FORUM POSTING

To document a posting to a Web discussion forum, include the author's name; the title of the posting, in quotation marks; the date of the posting; the URL, in angle brackets; and the date of access, in parentheses.

60. Karel Arnaut and Hein Vanhee, "History Facing the Present: An Interview with Jan Vansina," 1 November 2001, <www2.h_net.msu.edu/~africa/africaforum/VansinaInterview.htm> (5 February 2002).

EMAIL MESSAGE

Include the author's name; the author's email address; the subject line from the posting; the date of publication; the type of communication; and the date of access.

61. Kyla Berry, <kberry@aasc.mo.us> "Re: Newspaper Archives," 7 May 2000, personal email (8 May 2003).

LISTSERV OR NEWSGROUP MESSAGE

Include the author's name; the author's email address; the subject line from the posting; the date of publication; the name of the listserv or newsgroup; and the date of access.

62. Claire Dehon, <dehonel@ksu.edu> "Africa Forum: Heritage and History," 30 October 1998, <www.h-net.msu.edu> (10 December 1999).

SYNCHRONOUS COMMUNICATION

Include the speaker(s), if applicable; the title and date of the event, if appropriate; the type of communication; the source; the address; and the date of communication.

63. Jack Rauthier, personal communication, The Mud Connector MUD, <mud.theinquisition.net.5000> (3 May 2000).

7d-2. Models for bibliography entries

Your bibliography is a list of the books, articles, and other sources you used in preparing your paper. It must include all the works you cited in your notes; it may also include other works that you consulted but did not cite. However, avoid the temptation to pad your bibliography; list only materials you did in fact use.

You should list works in your bibliography alphabetically by authors' last names. If your bibliography is long, you may wish to divide it into sections. You might, for example, create separate headings such as "Primary Sources" and "Books and Articles." If you have used manuscripts or other unpublished sources, you might list these separately as well.

Books

A typical bibliography entry for a book contains the following information:

- The author's full name, last name first, followed by a period;
- The full title of the book, italicized or underlined, followed by a period;
- The city of publication, followed by a colon;
- The name of the publisher, followed by a comma;
- The date of publication, followed by a period.

Typically, the first line of a bibliography entry is typed flush left, and subsequent lines are indented. Individual entries should be single-spaced; double-space between entries.

Documentation Models for Bibliography Entries

Source

BASIC FORM FOR A BOOK

Waterman, Jonathan. *Arctic Crossing: A Journey through the Northwest Passage and Innuit Culture.* New York: Alfred A. Knopf, 2001.

MULTIPLE WORKS BY THE SAME AUTHOR

If your bibliography includes more than one work by the same author, you should use three dashes (or three hyphens) followed by a period (---.) in place of the author's name in subsequent bibliographic entries.

Waterman, Jonathan. *Arctic Crossing: A Journey through the Northwest Passage and Innuit Culture.* New York: Alfred A. Knopf, 2001.

---. *In the Shadow of Denali: Life and Death on Alaska's Mt. McKinley.* Guilford, Conn.: Lyons Press, 1998.

TWO OR MORE AUTHORS

An entry for a book with two or more authors should begin with the name of the first author listed on the title page, last name first. The names of the other authors are given in normal order.

Bradley, James, and Ron Powers. *Flags of Our Fathers.* New York: Bantam Books, 2000.

NOTE: For books with more than three authors, you may use the first author's name followed by the Latin term "et al." ("and others") in place of the other authors' names (for example, "Doe, Jane, et al.").

AUTHOR'S NAME IN THE TITLE

Begin the bibliography entry with the author's name, even if it appears in the title.

Darwin, Charles. *Charles Darwin's Letters: A Selection, 1825–1859.* Edited by Frederick Burkhardt. Cambridge: Cambridge University Press, 1996.

ANONYMOUS WORK

If the author of a work is unknown, list the work in the bibliography by its title. If the title begins with an article (*A, An,* or *The*), alphabetize the book according to the first letter of the next word.

DK Atlas of World History. New York: Dorling Kindersley, 2000.

EDITED OR COMPILED WORK WITHOUT AN AUTHOR

List a book by the last name of the editor, translator, or compiler if no author appears on the title page (as in a collection or anthology).

Freeze, Gregory L., ed. *Russia: A History*. New York: Oxford University Press, 2000.

EDITED WORK WITH AN AUTHOR

For a book with an author as well as an editor, the editor's name follows the title.

Karsh, Efraim. *Empires of the Sand: The Struggle for Mastery in the Middle East, 1789–1923*. Edited by Inari Karsh. Cambridge: Harvard University Press, 1999.

An entry for a book with multiple editors should be treated the same way as a book with multiple authors; list the editors in the order in which they appear on the title page. The first editor's last name should be given first, with names of subsequent editors given in the normal order.

Levine, Robert M., and John L. Crocitti, eds. *The Brazil Reader: History, Culture, Politics*. Durham, N.C.: Duke University Press, 1999.

TRANSLATED WORK

A translator's name, like an editor's, is placed after the title when an author's name is given. If a source has an editor and a translator, both should be listed.

Bingying, Xie. *A Woman Soldier's Own Story*. Translated by Barry Brissman and Lily Chia Brissman. New York: Columbia University Press, 2001.

MULTIVOLUME WORK

For a multivolume work, include the number of volumes in the bibliography entry.

Freedom: A Documentary History of Emancipation, 1861–1867. 4 vols. New York: Cambridge University Press, 1993.

If you have used a single volume of a multivolume set, cite only that volume. You can do this by giving the name of the volume first:

The Wartime Genesis of Free Labor: The Upper South. Edited by Ira Berlin. Vol. 1 of *Freedom: A Documentary History of Emancipation, 1861–1867.* New York: Cambridge University Press, 1993.

or by giving the name of the series first:

Freedom: A Documentary History of Emancipation, 1861–1867. Vol. 1, *The Wartime Genesis of Free Labor: The Upper South.* Edited by Ira Berlin. New York: Cambridge University Press, 1993.

If an individual volume in a multivolume work does not have its own title, specify the volume by number.

Cambridge History of American Foreign Relations. Vol. 1. Cambridge: Cambridge University Press, 1993.

If the volume or collection of volumes has an author, the entry should begin with the author's name (last name first), followed by a period.

ARTICLE OR DOCUMENT IN A COLLECTION OR ANTHOLOGY

List an article or document in a collection or anthology by the author of the article. You may include the pages on which the article begins and ends.

Huxley, Thomas H. "The Darwinian Hypothesis." In *Galileo's Commandment: An Anthology of Great Science Writing,* edited by Edmund Blair Bolles. New York: W. H. Freeman, 1997, 257–266.

CHAPTER IN AN EDITED WORK

When you are citing a book that has an editor or multiple editors, but in which the chapters have individual authors, you should cite the author and title of the chapter first, followed by the title, editor, and publication information for the book.

Prins, Harold E. L. "Children of Gluskap: Wabanaki Indians on the Eve of the European Invasion." In *American Beginnings: Exploration, Culture, and Cartography in the Land of Norumbega,* edited by Emerson W. Baker et al. Lincoln and London: University of Nebraska Press, 1994.

LETTER IN A PUBLISHED COLLECTION

If you cite only one letter from a collection, you may list it as an individual letter in your bibliography.

An Expectant Mother to Eleanor Roosevelt, 2 January 1935. In *America 1900–1999: Letters of the Century*. Edited by Lisa Grunwald and Stephen J. Adler. New York: Dial Press, 1999.

However, if you cite several letters from the same collection, list only the collection.

America 1900–1999: Letters of the Century. Edited by Lisa Grunwald and Stephen J. Adler. New York: Dial Press, 1999.

EDITION OTHER THAN THE FIRST

If you are using any edition other than the first, include the edition number in your bibliography.

Chafe, William H. *The Unfinished Journey: America since World War II*, 5th ed. New York: Oxford University Press, 2002.

WORK IN A SERIES

A series is a set of publications on the same general subject that is supervised by an editor or group of editors. Begin the entry with the author and title of the individual work from the series. Also include the title and editor of the series.

Abzug, Robert H. *America Views the Holocaust, 1933–1945*. Bedford Series in History and Culture, edited by (advisors) Natalie Zemon Davis and Ernest R. May. Boston: Bedford/St. Martin's, 1999.

Periodicals

A typical bibliography entry for an article in a journal includes the following information:

- The author's full name, last name first, followed by a period;
- The title of the article, in quotation marks and followed by a period;
- The name of the journal, italicized or underlined;
- The volume number, in arabic numerals;
- The date, in parentheses, followed by a colon;
- The pages on which the article begins and ends, followed by a period.

ARTICLE IN A JOURNAL PAGINATED BY VOLUME

Most scholarly journals are paginated consecutively throughout the volume. When citing an article from such a journal, it is not mandatory that you give the issue number.

Landsman, Ned C. "Nation, Migration, and the Province in the First British Empire: Scotland and the Americas, 1600–1800." *American Historical Review* 104 (1999): 463.

ARTICLE IN A JOURNAL PAGINATED BY ISSUE

If a journal paginates each issue separately, you must provide the issue number.

Wynn, Rhoda. "Saints and Sinners: Women and the Practice of Medicine throughout the Ages." *Journal of the American Medical Association* 283, no. 5 (2000): 668.

NOTE: If you wish to include the month of publication, put it before the year: (March 2000). If you include the month, you do not need the issue number.

ARTICLE IN A POPULAR MAGAZINE

It is not necessary to give the volume number or issue number for an article in a popular magazine. If you include page numbers, they are preceded by a comma, not by a colon.

Thomas, Evan. "The Day That Changed America." Newsweek Special Double Issue, December 2001–January 2002, 45–46.

NEWSPAPER ARTICLE

If you consulted various articles from a particular newspaper, you don't have to list the articles separately in the bibliography. Instead, provide just the name of the paper and the range of dates of the issues you consulted.

New York Times, September 2002–January 2003.

BOOK REVIEW

List a book review by the reviewer's last name. If the author of the review is not named, begin with the title of the review or, if the review is untitled, with the words "Review of."

Cooper, Ilene. Review of *Nat Turner's Slave Rebellion in American History,* by Judith Edwards. *Booklist* 96 (2000): 1093.

Review of *A Middle East Mosaic: Fragments of Life, Letters and History,* edited by Bernard Lewis. *Publishers Weekly,* 24 March 2000, 80.

Public documents

The same information should be provided as for notes (see pp. 93–96). In a paper on United States history, you may omit "United States" or "U.S." as the country in which a document was issued if it is clear in context.

PRESIDENTIAL PAPERS

Entries for these papers often begin with and are alphabetized by the president's name.

Eisenhower, Dwight D. *Public Papers of the Presidents of the United States: Dwight D. Eisenhower, 1953.* Washington, D.C.: GPO, 1960.

EXECUTIVE DEPARTMENT DOCUMENT

Entries for these documents begin with the issuing department's name.

U.S. General Accounting Office. *Desert Shield and Desert Storm Reports and Testimonies, 1991–93.* Washington, D.C.: General Accounting Office, 1994.

U.S. Department of State. *Belarus.* Background Notes Series, no. 10344.

TESTIMONY BEFORE A COMMITTEE

If you cite or consult a transcript of testimony before a committee, begin the entry with the name of the committee.

Senate Committee on Foreign Relations. Countering the Changing Threat of International Terrorism: Report of the National Commission on Terrorism: Hearing before the Committee on Foreign Relations. 106th Cong., 2nd sess., 2000.

CONGRESSIONAL COMMITTEE PRINT

Entries for these research reports should include the print number or date.

U.S. Congress, House Committee on International Relations. International Terrorism: A Compilation of Major Laws, Treaties, Agreements, and Executive Documents. 106th Cong., 2nd sess., 2000. Committee Print.

TREATY

Begin the entry with the name of the issuing agency.

U.S. Department of State. "Jay Treaty," 19 November 1794. TIAS no. 105. *United States Treaties and Other International Agreements,* vol. 2.

(See p. 95 for information about the TIAS number.)

UNITED STATES CONSTITUTION

If you cite the Constitution in your paper, you *do not* need to include it in your bibliography.

Other sources

UNPUBLISHED THESIS OR DISSERTATION

List an unpublished thesis or dissertation by its author's last name.

Nemes, Robert James."Between Reform and Revolution: Associations, Culture, and Politics in Budapest, 1800–1849." Ph.D. diss., Columbia University, 1999.

UNPUBLISHED LETTER IN A MANUSCRIPT COLLECTION

If you have used material from manuscript collections, the bibliography entry should begin with the specific item, followed by its location. For a letter, start with the name of the author of the collected manuscripts or the title of the collection, followed by the depository and its location.

Beekman, James W. *Papers.* New-York Historical Society, New York.

If you have only cited one item from the collection, list it under the name of the author.

Hawthorne, Nathaniel. Letter to James W. Beekman. *James W. Beekman Papers.* New-York Historical Society, New York.

ILLUSTRATION OR MAP

For an illustration or map in a printed text, give the author, title, city, publisher, and year.

Time/CBS News. *People of the Century.* New York: Simon & Schuster, 1999.

Mignolo, Walter D. *The Darker Side of the Renaissance: Literacy, Territoriality, and Colonization.* Ann Arbor: University of Michigan Press, 1995.

SOUND RECORDING

List a sound recording by the composer's last name or, for a collection or an anonymous work, by the title of the recording. Include the recording company and number if they are provided.

Holst, Gustav. *The Planets.* Royal Philharmonic Orchestra. André Previn. Telarc compact disc 80133.

Virtuoso Recorder Music. Amsterdam Loeki Stardust Quartet. Decca compact disc 414 277-2.

FILM, VIDEOCASSETTE, OR DVD

After the film title, include the name of the producer and director, the playing time, the production company, the date, and the medium.

The Civil War. Produced by Ken Burns. 11 hours. PBS Video, 1990. 9 videocassettes.

INTERVIEW

List an interview under the name of the person interviewed and provide the date of the interview.

McVeigh, Timothy. Interviewed by Ed Bradley. *60 Minutes.* Columbia Broadcasting System, 26 March 2000.

PERSONAL COMMUNICATION

Because your reader will not have access to personal interviews you conducted or letters you received, you *do not* need to list these sources of information in your bibliography.

REFERENCE WORKS AND THE BIBLE

Well-known reference works and the Bible are usually *not* included in bibliographies.

INDIRECT SOURCE

If material you have taken from one source originally appeared in another source and you have not consulted the original yourself, your bibliography entry should begin with the original source but must include your own source for the information. The page numbers from both sources should be included.

Knoles, George Harmon. *The Jazz Age Revisited: British Criticism of American Civilization during the 1920s,* 31. Stanford: Stanford University Press, 1955. Quoted in C. Vann

Woodward, *The Old World's New World* (Oxford: Oxford University Press, 1991), 46.

Electronic sources

WHOLE WEB SITE WITH A KNOWN AUTHOR

Bibliographic entries for a complete Web site with a known author should begin with the author's last name. Periods, rather than commas, are used to separate the elements of the entry.

Elliston, Jon. *The Bay of Pigs Invasion.* 1996. <www.parascope.com/articles/1296/bayofpigs.htm> (5 August 2002).

WHOLE WEB SITE WITH AN UNKNOWN AUTHOR

If you are citing a Web site whose authorship is unknown, begin with the title of the Web site. Use periods in place of commas to separate the title, date, and URL.

Military History On-Line. 2000. <www.militaryhistoryonline.com/> (4 July 2000).

SELECTION FROM A WEB SITE

To cite a selection from a Web site, begin with the last name of the author of the selection (if known). Separate the elements of the citation with periods.

Linder, Douglas. "An Account of Events in Salem." *Famous Trials.* June 2001. <www.law.umkc.edu/faculty/projects/ftrials/salem/sal_acct.htm> (23 September 2002).

ONLINE BOOK

A bibliographic citation for an online book should begin with the last name of the author of the book. If you access an online book through an authored Web site, also include the author, name, and date of the Web site, if known.

Wallace, Alfred Russell. *The Malay Archipelago.* 1869. Project Gutenberg. February 2001. <ftp://ibiblio.org/pub/docs/books/gutenberg/etext01/1malay10.txt> (6 January 2003).

Mather, Cotton. *Memorable Providences, Relating to Witchcrafts and Possessions.* Boston: 1689. At Douglas Linder. *Famous Trials.* 2002. <www.law.umkc.edu/faculty/projects/ftrials/salem/asa_math.htm> (22 October 2002).

ARTICLE IN AN ELECTRONIC JOURNAL

A citation for an article in an electronic journal should begin with the author's last name. Elements of the entry should be separated by periods.

Lindly, Arthur. "The Ahistoricism of Medieval Film." *Screening the Past* 3 (1998). <www.latrobe.edu.au/screeningthepast/firstrelease/fir598/ALfr3a.htm> (15 May 2001).

ARTICLE ACCESSED THROUGH AN ELECTRONIC DATABASE

To cite an article from a print journal accessed through an electronic database, include the information you would include for a journal article in print. Follow this by the name of the online database; the URL for the database, in angle brackets; and the date of access, in parentheses.

Toplin, Robert Brent. "The Filmmaker as Historian." *American Historical Review* 93 (1988): 1210–27. Online via JSTOR. <www.jstor.org/> (2 November 1999).

ONLINE GOVERNMENT PUBLICATION

A citation for a government publication should include the author's name, inverted, and followed by a period; the title of the document; the type of document; the date of publication; the URL, in angle brackets; and the date of access, in parentheses.

Bush, George W. "Creation of the President's Council on Bioethics." Executive Order, 28 November 2001. <www.whitehouse.gov/news/releases/2001/11/20011128_13.html> (17 October 2002).

ONLINE NEWSPAPER ARTICLE

To cite an online newspaper article, begin with the author's last name, if known; the title of the article; the name of the newspaper; the date of publication; the URL, in angle brackets; and the date of access, in parentheses. All elements of the entry should be separated by periods.

Nakashima, Ellen, and Alan Sipress. "Bali Bombing Suspect Linked to Allies of Al Qaeda." *Washington Post.com.* 11 November 2002. <www.washingtonpost.com/wp_dyn/articles/A37002_2002Nov10.html> (29 December 2002).

ONLINE REVIEW

A citation for an online review should begin with the last name of the reviewer; the title and author of the book being reviewed; the name of the online publication; the date of the review; the URL, in angle brackets; and the date of access, in parentheses. The elements of the entry should be separated by periods.

Schmemann, Serge. Review of *Natasha's Dance*, by Orlando Figes. *New York Times on the Web*. 10 November 2002. <www.nytimes.com/2002/11/10/books/review/10SCHMEMT.html> (16 January 2003).

WEB DISCUSSION FORUM POSTING

To document a posting to a Web discussion forum, include the author's name, in reverse order; the title of the posting, in quotation marks; the date of the posting; the URL, in angle brackets; and the date of access, in parentheses. Use periods to separate the elements in the entry.

Arnaut, Karel, and Hein Vanhee. "History Facing the Present: An Interview with Jan Vansina." 1 November 2001. <www2.h_net.msu.edu/~africa/africaforum/VansinaInterview.htm> (5 February 2002).

EMAIL MESSAGE

Berry, Kyla. <kberry@aasc.mo.us> "Re: Newspaper Archives," 7 May 2000. Personal email (8 May 2003).

LISTSERV OR NEWSGROUP MESSAGE

Dehon, Claire. <dehone1@ksu.edu> "Africa Forum: Heritage and History," 30 October 1998. <www.h-net.msu.edu> (10 December 1999).

SYNCHRONOUS COMMUNICATION

Rauthier, Jack. Personal communication. The Mud Connector MUD. <mud.theinquisition.net.5000> (3 May 2000).

7e. Sample pages from a student research paper

Most of the suggestions in this book have been directed toward a single end: the production of a carefully researched, well-organized, and clearly written paper. On the following pages, you will find the title page, opening paragraphs, notes, and bibliography for one such paper.

SAMPLE TITLE PAGE

To Try a Monarch:
The Trials and Executions of
Charles I of England and Louis XVI of France

by
Lynn Chandler

History 362
Dr. Joan Kinnaird
November 24, 2003

SAMPLE PAGE

Chandler 1

On January 30, 1649, Charles I, king of England, was beheaded.[1] The crowd around the scaffold greeted the sight of the severed head of their monarch with astonished silence. After lying in state for several days, the body was carried "in a Hearse covered with black Velvet, and drawn by six Horses, with four Coaches following it. . . ."[2] to Windsor Castle, where Charles was buried in royal estate beside Henry VIII and Queen Jane Seymour.[3] The scene was quite different on January 21, 1793, when another monarch ascended the scaffold--Louis XVI, king of the French. In place of the silence that followed Charles's execution, Louis's decapitation was announced with a "flourish of trumpets," and the executioner's cry of "Thus dies a Traitor!"[4] Contemporaries reported that the crowd surged forward, dipped their handkerchiefs in the king's blood, and ran through the streets shouting "Behold the Blood of a Tyrant!"[5] The body was wrapped in canvas and brought in a cart to the Tuileries, where Louis XVI, the former king of France, was buried like a commoner.[6] These two events, separated by almost a century and a half, appear at first glance to be totally isolated from each other. A careful review of both official documents and private accounts, however, reveals that the chief actors in the drama surrounding the execution of Louis XVI were not only aware of the English precedent, but referred to it again and again in the process of choosing their own courses of action, arguing for the validity of their point of view, and justifying their actions to the world.

The first clear-cut evidence that the French were influenced by the trial and execution of Charles I can be found in contemporary transcripts of the trial itself. In the debate surrounding the decision to execute the king, those who favored leniency often cited the English precedent to support their position.

SAMPLE ENDNOTES PAGE

Chandler 10

Notes

1. For a good general study of the execution, see Ann Hughes, "The Execution of Charles I," May 2001, www.bbc.co.uk/history/state/monarchs_leaders/charlesi_execution_1.shtml (21 October 2003).

2. *England's Black Tribunal: The Tryal of King Charles the First* (printed for C. Revington, at the Bible and Crown in St. Paul's Churchyard, 1737), 55.

3. For a detailed account of the trial and execution of Charles I, see C. V. Wedgwood, *A Coffin for King Charles: The Trial and Execution of Charles I* (New York: Time Incorporated, 1966) and Graham Edwards, *The Last Days of Charles I* (Stroud, Gloucestershire: Sutton Publishing, 1999).

4. Joseph Trapp, *The Trial of Louis XVI* (London, 1793), 205.

5. Trapp, 206.

6. Trapp, 145. For a detailed account of the trial and execution of Louis XVI, see David P. Jordan, *The King's Trial: The French Revolution vs. Louis XVI* (Berkeley and Los Angeles: University of California Press, 1979).

7. Michael Walzer, ed., *Regicide and Revolution: Speeches at the Trial of Louis XVI*, trans. Marian Rothstein (Cambridge: Cambridge University Press, 1974), 1–89 passim.

8. Patricia Crawford, "'Charles Stuart, That Man of Blood,'" *Journal of British Studies* 16, no. 2 (1977): 53.

9. Wedgwood, 89.

10. Susan Dunn, *The Deaths of Louis XVI: Regicide and the French Political Imagination* (Princeton, N.J.: Princeton University Press, 1994), 59.

11. Jordan, 122.

12. John Hardman, *The French Revolution Sourcebook* (London: Arnold Publishers, 1999), 178.

SAMPLE BIBLIOGRAPHY

Chandler 11

Bibliography

Blackwell, Freida H., and Jay Losey. "The Execution of Charles I: History and Perspectives." n.d. <www.baylor.edu/~BIC/WCIII/Essays/charles.1.html> (23 March 2000).

Crawford, Patricia. "'Charles Stuart, That Man of Blood.'" *Journal of British Studies* 16, no. 2 (1977): 41–61.

Dunn, Susan. *The Deaths of Louis XVI: Regicide and the French Political Imagination.* Princeton, N.J.: Princeton University Press, 1994.

Edwards, Graham. *The Last Days of Charles I.* Stroud Gloucestershire: Sutton Publishing, 1999.

England's Black Tribunal: The Tryal of King Charles the First. Printed for C. Revington, at the Bible and Crown in St. Paul's Churchyard, 1737.

Hardman, John. *The French Revolution Sourcebook.* London: Arnold Publishers, 1999.

Hughes, Ann. "The Execution of Charles I." May 2001. <www.bbc.co.uk/history/state/monarchs_leaders/charlesi_execution_1.shtml> (21 October 2003).

Jordan, David P. "In Defense of the King." *Stanford French Review* 1, no. 3 (1977): 325–38.

---. *The King's Trial: The French Revolution vs. Louis XVI.* Berkeley and Los Angeles: University of California Press, 1979.

Trapp, Joseph. *The Trial of Louis XVI.* London, 1793.

Walzer, Michael, ed. *Regicide and Revolution: Speeches at the Trial of Louis XVI.* Translated by Marian Rothstein. Cambridge: Cambridge University Press, 1974.

Wedgwood, C. V. *A Coffin for King Charles: The Trial and Execution of Charles I.* New York: Time Incorporated, 1966.

Appendix A
Writing Guides of Interest to Historians

The following books offer helpful guidance on stylistic matters and other writing concerns. The guides to writing in history, in addition to offering general advice, discuss how historians work and cover typical assignments, stylistic conventions, the research process, and documentation.

GENERAL WRITING GUIDES

Hacker, Diana. *A Pocket Style Manual.* 4th ed. Boston: Bedford/St. Martin's, 2004. Also available at <www.dianahacker.com/pocket>.

Hacker, Diana. *Rules for Writers.* 5th ed. Boston: Bedford/St. Martin's, 2004. Also available at <bedfordstmartins.com/hacker/rules>.

Strunk, William, Jr., and E. B. White. *The Elements of Style.* 4th ed. New York: Macmillan, 1999.

Turabian, Kate L., Alice Bennett, and John Grossman. *A Manual for Writers of Term Papers, Theses, and Dissertations.* 6th ed. Chicago: University of Chicago Press, 1996.

University of Chicago Press. *The Chicago Manual of Style.* 14th ed. Chicago: University of Chicago Press, 1993.

GUIDES TO WRITING IN HISTORY

Benjamin, Jules R. *A Student's Guide to History.* 9th ed. Boston: Bedford/St. Martin's, 2004. Also available at <bedfordstmartins.com/studentsguide>.

Hellstern, Mark, Gregory M. Scott, and Stephen M. Garrison. *The History Student Writer's Manual.* Upper Saddle River, N.J.: Prentice Hall, 1997.

Marius, Richard, and Melvin E. Page. *A Short Guide to Writing about History.* 4th ed. New York: Pearson Education, 2001.

Storey, William Kelleher. *Writing History: A Guide for Students.* New York: Oxford University Press, 1998.

INTERNET GUIDES FOR HISTORIANS

Harnack, Andrew, and Eugene Kleppinger. *Online! A Reference Guide to Using Internet Sources.* 4th ed. Boston: Bedford/St. Martin's, 2001. Also available at <bedfordstmartins.com/online>.

Reagan, Patrick. *Guide to History and the Internet.* Boston: McGraw-Hill, 2002.

Trinkle, Dennis A., and Scott A. Merriman. *The European History Highway: A Guide to Internet Resources.* Armonk, N.Y.: M. E. Sharpe. 2002.

Trinkle, Dennis A., and Scott A. Merriman. *The History Highway 3.0: A Guide to Internet Resources.* 3rd ed. Armonk, N.Y.: M. E. Sharpe. 2002.

Appendix B
Guide to Resources in History

by Susan Craig, Trinity College

While conducting research in history, you will need to collect evidence and find commentary that helps you interpret it. The library and the Internet both offer tools that can help you track down primary and secondary sources and answer questions that arise as you learn more about your chosen topic. This appendix suggests selected print indexes, references, periodicals, and sources of primary documents, as well as a sampler of electronic sources available through the Internet.

Library resources

The materials listed here may not be available at all libraries, but they give you an idea of the range of resources available. Remember, too, that librarians are an extremely helpful resource; they know their own collections well and can direct you to useful materials throughout your research process.

INDEXES

America: History and Life. Santa Barbara, Calif.: ABC-CLIO, 1964–.
Article abstract on the history of the U.S. and Canada published throughout the world, as well as articles dealing with current U.S. culture. Includes book reviews and dissertation abstracts. Available in print, on CD-ROM, and online.

Historical Abstracts. Santa Barbara, Calif.: ABC-CLIO, 1955–.
Abstracts from world periodical literature covering world history from 1450, excluding the U.S. and Canada. From 1971, selectively indexes book reviews, monographs, and dissertations. Available in print, CD-ROM, and online.

GUIDES AND BIBLIOGRAPHIES

American Historical Association's Guide to Historical Literature. 3rd ed. New York: Oxford University Press, 1995.
Over 27,000 citations, arranged in sections covering theory and international history, and regional history. Updated to include current trends in historical research.

Encyclopedia of Historians and Historical Writing. Chicago: Fitzroy Dearborn, 1999.

A two-volume international guide to influential historians and historical debates. Includes biographies of individuals born before 1945, essays on nations and geographical regions, and topical essays.

United States History: A Selective Guide to Information Sources. Englewood, Col.: Libraries Unlimited, 1994.

Over 1,000 topically-arranged annotated entries describe reference, bibliographic, and biographical sources.

TOPICAL OVERVIEWS AND ENCYCLOPEDIAS

North and South America

Cambridge History of the Native Peoples of the Americas. Cambridge: Cambridge University Press, 1996.

A three-volume set, organized into thematic and regional chapters. Includes maps and photographs.

Encyclopedia of African-American Culture and History. New York: Macmillan Library Reference, 1996.

A five-volume set with entries that cover people, places, events, concepts, and topics.

Encyclopedia of Japanese American History: An A-to-Z Reference from 1868 to the Present. Rev. ed. New York: Facts on File, 2001.

Contains a historical overview, a chronology, and entries describing events, people, organizations, and communities. Includes photographs and illustrations.

Encyclopedia of Latin American History and Culture. New York: Scribner's, 1996.

Over 5,000 entries in five volumes. Includes illustrations.

Encyclopedia of Mexico: History, Society, and Culture. Chicago: Fitzroy Dearborn Publishers, 1997.

This two-volume set provides bibliographic and factual data on historical figures, events, and institutions. Includes maps and a thematic outline of entries.

Encyclopedia of the American Civil War: A Political, Social, and Military History. Santa Barbara, Calif.: ABC-CLIO, 2000.

This five-volume set covers people, places, and events. Includes a list of maps, illustrations, photographs, glossary, suggestions for further reading, primary documents, chronology, and lists of U.S. and Confederate officers.

Encyclopedia of the Confederacy. New York: Simon & Schuster, 1993.

A four-volume set that covers battles, campaigns, events, society, culture, politics, and prominent Confederate individuals. Includes illustrations and maps.

Encyclopedia of the North American Colonies. New York: Simon & Schuster, 1993.

A three-volume set that covers politics, education, religion, economics, social issues, people, and events in topical sections. Includes illustrations and maps.

Encyclopedia of the United States in the Twentieth Century. New York: Scribner's, 1996.

This four-volume set covers U.S. cultural, social, and intellectual history. Includes maps, cross-references, and a bibliography. A supplement volume includes a topical chronology from 1898 to 1995.

Encyclopedia of the Vietnam War: A Political, Social, and Military History. Santa Barbara, Calif.: ABC-CLIO, 1998.

This three-volume set details Vietnamese history, including French and U.S. involvement. Includes maps, illustrations, and key documents.

Encyclopedia of Women's History in America. 2nd ed. New York: Facts on File, 2000.

Topical and biographical entries of women central to U.S. cultural, intellectual, and political history. Includes documents.

Facts on File Encyclopedia of Black Women in America. New York: Facts on File, 1997.

This eleven-volume set covers literature, arts, sports, business, education, religion, law, science, and health. Includes illustrations, photographs, and an occupational index.

Longman Companion to America in the Era of the Two World Wars. 1910–1945. London: Harlow, 1996.

Collects chronological, statistical, and tabular data covering political, social, and economic history, as well as biographies. Includes genealogies and maps.

Worldwide

Africana: The Encyclopedia of the African and African American Experience. New York: Basic Civitas Books, 1999.

Articles on the history of each African nation and major cultural, political, and religious movement in Africa and the U.S.

Civilizations of the Ancient Near East. New York: Scribner's, 1995.

This four-volume set includes a "Timetable of Civilizations," illustrations, and maps.

Encyclopedia of Eastern Europe from the Congress of Vienna to the Fall of Communism. New York: Garland, 2002.

Focuses on developments over the past two centuries and addresses geography, history, government, economy, culture, trends, and ideas. Includes maps and suggestions for further reading.

Encyclopedia of Pre-colonial Africa: Archaeology, History, Languages, Cultures, and Environments. Walnut Creek, Calif.: Alta Mira Press, 1997.

An encyclopedia with topical articles surveys sub-Saharan African culture through time. Includes suggestions for further reading, maps, illustrations, and figures.

Encyclopedia of Russian History: From the Christianization of Kiev to the Break-up of the USSR. Santa Barbara, Calif.: ABC-CLIO, 1993.

Contains over 2,500 entries covering people, places, religious and political movements, intellectual ideas, and the arts.

Encyclopedia of the Holocaust. New York: Macmillan, 1990.
Documents the background, history, and impact of the Holocaust. Includes illustrations, photographs and maps.

Encyclopedia of the Renaissance. New York: Scribner's, 1999.
This six-volume set covers cultural, historical, and individual achievements. Includes a chronology, illustrations, and color plates.

Encyclopedia of the Wars of the Roses. Santa Barbara, Calif.: ABC-CLIO, 2001.
Describes people, events, and terms. Includes illustrations, maps, suggestions for further reading, a chronology and lists of genealogies, selected historical fiction, and selected Web sites.

Historical Encyclopedia of the Arab-Israeli Conflict. Westport, Conn.: Greenwood Press, 1996.
Covers important political, military, and diplomatic events, places, people, treaties, and issues. Includes suggestions for further reading, and a chronology of events.

Holocaust Encyclopedia. New Haven, Conn.: Yale University Press, 2001.
This work by scholars and eyewitnesses includes a chronology, illustration, and photographs.

Longman Handbook of Early Modern Europe, 1453–1763. London: Harlow, 2001.
Collects chronological, statistical, and tabular data covering political, social, and economic history. Includes genealogies.

Longman Handbook of Modern British History, 1714–2001. 4th ed. London: Harlow, 2001.
Collects chronological, statistical, and tabular data covering political, social, and economic history. Includes genealogies and a glossary.

Longman Handbook of Modern European History, 1763–1997. 3rd ed. London: Harlow, 1998.
Collects chronological, statistical, and tabular data covering political, social, and economic history. Includes genealogies and maps.

Macmillan Encyclopedia of World Slavery. New York: Macmillan Reference, 1998.
This two-volume set documents the institution of slavery on a global scale, from ancient times to the present.

Medieval England: An Encyclopedia. New York: Garland, 1998.
An introduction to English society and culture, with illustrations, photographs, maps, bibliographies, glossary, lists of kings, queens, and popes.

Middle East. 9th ed. Washington, D.C.: CQ Press, 2000.
An overview of the Middle East covering the Arab-Israeli conflict, U.S. policy, Persian Gulf, oil, Islam, and country profiles. Includes maps, tables, documents, and a chronology.

Middle East and North Africa 2002. 48th ed. London: Europa Publications, 2001.

A survey with chapters on each country covering geography, history, economy, politics, and government, and a bibliography for further reading also includes nine general survey articles.

Modern Germany: An Encyclopedia of History, People, and Culture, 1871–1990. New York: Garland, 1998.

A two-volume set covers Germany from its political unification to the fall of the Berlin Wall, looking at key people, places, events, institutions, and issues. Includes illustrations, maps, and a subject guide.

Oxford Encyclopedia of the Modern Islamic World. New York: Oxford University Press, 1995.

This four-volume set offers articles on all facets of Muslim historical, social, political, and religious life.

Oxford History of Britain. Oxford: Oxford University Press, 1992.

A five-volume set arranged chronologically. Includes maps, illustrations, and a genealogy.

Oxford History of Christianity. Oxford: Oxford University Press, 1993.

Covers religious, cultural, and political events. Includes illustrations, maps, and suggestions for further reading.

Tudor England: An Encyclopedia. New York: Garland, 2001.

Entries introduce key personalities, history, religion, art, music, politics, science, society, and literature. Includes a chronology.

SPECIALIZED DICTIONARIES

United States

ABC-CLIO Companion to Women's Progress in America. Santa Barbara, Calif.: ABC-CLIO, 1994.

A record of milestones of women's history since 1619.

Dictionary of American Biography. New York: Cambridge University Press, 1995.

This multivolume work provides biographical entries of significant Americans.

Historical Dictionary of the American Revolution. Lanham, Md.: Scarecrow Press, 1999.

Includes topical entries, and key military and political documents.

Worldwide

Blackwell Companion to the Enlightenment. Oxford: Blackwell, 1995.

Entries on music, art, literature, technological advances, and key personalities from around the world.

Dictionary of Ancient History. Oxford: Blackwell, 1994.

Entries on personalities, events, literature, philosophy, art, religions, and sciences in the Greco-Roman world.

Dictionary of Concepts in History. New York: Greenwood, 1996.

Essays that define historiographic concepts and describe how the concepts were formed. Contains excellent bibliographies.

Dictionary of Eighteenth-Century World History. Oxford: Blackwell, 1994.

References key people, events, movements, and institutions and covers historical, political, military, social, economic, and cultural issues. Includes bibliographical references, maps, and a chronology.

Dictionary of Modern Arab History: An A–Z of Over 2000 Entries from 1798 to the Present Day. London: Kegan Paul International, 1998.

References key people, history, politics, diplomacy, commerce, strategic studies, and culture of Arab lands.

Dictionary of Nineteenth-Century World History. Oxford: Blackwell, 1994.

References key events and personalities and covers historical, political, military, social, economic, and cultural issues. Includes bibliographical references, maps, and chronology.

Dictionary of the Middle Ages. New York: Scribner's, 1982–89.

This thirteen-volume set covers people, events, ideas, movements, texts, and cultural features of the medieval world (A.D. 500–1500).

Dictionary of the Middle East. New York: St. Martin's Press, 1996.

Covers key personalities, places of religious and cultural significance, natural resources, political and religious sects, and economics. Includes maps.

Dictionary of Twentieth-Century World History. New York: Oxford University Press, 1997.

Topical and biographical entries of sovereign countries, historical regions, world and military leaders, movements, and treaties.

Historical Dictionary of Germany. Metuchen, N.J.: Scarecrow Press, 1994.

Introduces key people, places, events, and cultural developments. Includes chronology, an extensive bibliography, maps, and illustrations.

Historical Dictionary of the Elizabethan World: Britain, Ireland, Europe, and America. Phoenix, Ariz.: Oryx Press, 1999.

Entries on people, events, ideas, and terms. Contains genealogies; lists of archbishops, monarchs, and popes; historical literature, motion pictures, and sound recordings; Web sites; and a chronology.

One Europe, Many Nations: A Historical Dictionary of European National Groups. Westport, Conn.: Greenwood Press, 2000.

Addresses Europeans as distinct national groups and follows each group's development. Entries include the flag, map, geographical location, national characteristics, and historical development. Includes a list of European language groups.

Oxford Companion to Military History. Oxford: Oxford University Press, 2001.

Covers battles, military concepts, weapons, uniforms, equipment, casualties, politics, and gender. Includes maps, and illustrations.

ATLASES, CHRONOLOGIES, AND TIMETABLES

North and South America

Atlas of American History. Rev. and updated. New York: Facts on File, 1995.

Offers articles, maps, photographs, and illustrations.

Black Saga: The African-American Experience — A Chronology. Washington, D.C.: Civitas/Counterpoint, 1999.

A chronological documentary of African American history.

Chronology of Hispanic-American History. New York: Gale, 1995.

Lists historical and cultural highlights. Includes regional histories and significant documents.

Chronology of Native American History from Pre-Columbian Times to the Present. Detroit: Gale, 1994.

List of historical and cultural events involving the native peoples of North America and Canada. Includes illustrations, a list of American Indian orators, historical documents, and excerpts from significant legal cases.

Historic Atlas of Canada. Toronto: University of Toronto Press, 1987–93.

This three-volume set covers historical, social, and economic evolution. Includes maps, illustrations, primary and secondary sources, and suggestions for further reading.

This Day in American History. Rev. ed. Jefferson, N.C.: McFarland, 2001.

Describes key events for each day.

Wars of the Americas: A Chronology of Armed Conflict in the New World, 1492 to the Present. Santa Barbara, Calif.: ABC-CLIO, 1998.

Describes armed conflicts. Includes suggestions for further reading, photographs, illustrations, and maps.

Worldwide

Atlas of Classical History. New York: Oxford University Press, 1994.

Maps cover the Near East, ancient Egypt, Greece, and Rome.

Atlas of World History. New York: Oxford University Press, 1999.

Chronological and regional sections describe the important themes with narrative text. Includes time charts; gazetteer of events, people, and places; maps; and illustrations.

Chronology of European History: 15,000 B.C. to 1997. Pasadena, Calif.: Salem Press, 1997.

Chronological entries on social, political, economic, and intellectual history.

Chronology of Twentieth-Century Eastern Europe History. Detroit: Gale, 1994.

Covers major political, economic, and cultural events, arranged by countries.

Chronology of Women's History. Westport, Conn.: Greenwood, 1994.

Chronological entries highlight the landmarks in women's history.

Chronology of World History. Santa Barbara, Calif.: ABC-CLIO, 1999.

This four-volume set includes entries arranged chronologically and grouped into topical categories.

Chronology of World Slavery. Santa Barbara, Calif.: ABC-CLIO, 1999.

Examines slavery throughout history and across cultures with topical articles and a collection of primary documents.

Columbia Chronologies of Asian History and Culture. New York: Columbia University Press, 2000.

A chronology of politics, history, arts, culture, thought, religion, science and technology, economics, and everyday life.

Encyclopedic World Atlas: A–Z Country-by-Country Coverage. 5th ed. New York: Oxford University Press, 2000.

Provides maps of the world, continents, and countries. Articles on each country describes geography, climate, history, politics, economy, and population.

Historic World Leaders. Detroit: Gale, 1994.

This five-volume set offers over 620 biographical sketches of world leaders. Each entry includes an illustration or photograph, a chronology, vital statistics, biographical profile, and suggestions for further reading. Each volume includes maps and a chronology of leaders by geographic area.

Historical Atlas of Britain. Dover, N.H.: A. Sutton, in association with the National Trust, 1994.

Includes topical essays, maps, and illustrations.

Rand McNally Atlas of World History. Chicago: Rand McNally, 1995.

Shows the development of human society in its physical setting through maps and text.

Smithsonian Timelines of the Ancient World. New York: Dorling Kindersley, 1993.

Provides geographical charts, introductory historical text, and topical articles.

Times Atlas of European History. New York: Times Books, 1994.

Includes maps and short narratives.

Wilson Calendar of World History. New York: H. W. Wilson, 1999.

This chronology divides geographic regions and the topical areas of science, invention, and technology; religion; and culture and arts. Includes illustrations.

Where to find primary sources

There are many places to find primary sources for historical research. You can search your library catalog or consult anthologies of documents covering particular themes or periods in history. Many Web sites also offer primary source material. The following materials can help you as well.

THE PRESS

African American History in the Press, 1851–1899. Detroit: Gale, 1996.

Chronologically arranged articles, editorials, and cartoons from major newspapers provide a look at positive and negative portrayals of African Americans.

Herstory. Berkeley, Calif.: Women's History Research Center, 1972, 1976.

Microfilm collection of alternative feminist periodicals published between 1956 and 1974. Offers documentary history of the women's movement.

The New York Times. New York: H. J. Raymond, 1851–.

Many libraries have this newspaper on microfilm going back to the first issue in 1851. Available online at <www.nytimes.com> and through UMI ProQuest Historical Newspaper Database at many libraries.

The Times. London: Times Newspapers, 1788–.

This newspaper is available in microfilm at some libraries. An index covers the *Times* and its predecessor, the *Daily Universal Register,* from 1785 to the present. Available online at <www.the-times.co.uk>.

DIARIES, PAMPHLETS, AND BOOKS

Afro-American Pamphlets. Pts. 1–3, 1827–1948.

A set of 149 pamphlets by influential African Americans of educational, political, and social significance.

American Culture Series.

A microfilm set, featuring books and pamphlets published between 1493 and 1875.

American Diaries: An Annotated Bibliography of Published American Diaries and Journals. Detroit: Gale, 1983, 1987. Vol. 1, Diaries, Written 1492–1864 (1983). Vol. 2, Diaries, Written 1865–1980 (1987).

Over 6,000 entries from all fifty states and Spanish American sites arranged chronologically and then alphabetically by author.

American Women's Diaries from the Collection of the American Antiquarian Society. New Canaan, Conn.: Readex Corp., 1984–.

A set of microfilmed diaries kept by women.

Early English Books, 1475–1640. Early English Books, 1641–1700. Ann Arbor, Mich.: UMI Press, 1987–.

A vast collection of early books on microfilm.

PUBLIC DOCUMENTS

Many libraries house collections of state, federal, and United Nations documents. These papers can provide detailed records of public life. If your library does not have a documents collection, you might be able to borrow documents from a regional depository. The following are some useful series.

CIS U.S. Serial Set, 1789–1969. Washington, D.C.: Congressional Information Service, 1975–79.

A compilation of congressional documents, beginning with the first session of Congress. Some libraries have this set in microfiche.

Congressional Record. Washington, D.C.: GPO, 1873–.

Covers debates and proceedings of Congress. Earlier series were called *Debates and Proceedings* (*Annals of Congress, Register of Debates,* and *Congressional Globe*). Also available on microfilm, on CD-ROM, and online at <www.access.gpo.gov>.

Foreign Relations of the United States. Diplomatic Papers. Washington, D.C.: GPO, 1861–.

A collection of documents, including diplomatic papers, correspondence, and memoranda, that provides a detailed record of U.S. foreign policy. Some documents are available online at <www.state.gov/r/pa/ho/frus/>.

Hansard's Parliamentary Debates. Great Britain.

Proceedings of the English Parliament, with the text of debates in the House of Commons and the House of Lords. The full text of many recent debates since 1988 is available online at <www.publications.parliament.uk/pa/cm/cmhansrd.htm>.

Journals of the Continental Congress, 1774–1789. Washington, D.C.: National Archives and Records Service, 1904–37. 34 vols.

Papers of the Continental Congress, 1774–1779. Washington, D.C.: National Archives and Records Service, 1959. 204 microfilm reels.

Public Papers of the Presidents of the United States. Washington, D.C.: GPO, 1909–.

Includes major documents issued by the executive branch since Hoover's administration. Many sets of papers from earlier presidencies have been published as well.

LOCAL HISTORY COLLECTIONS

Local historical societies often house a wealth of documents. While using their resources, you may find that you are the first to work with their materials.

Internet Search Tools

SEARCH ENGINES

Search engines are programs that locate Internet sources containing the search terms you provide. Because they seek matches based exclusively on the words you enter and don't screen for quality, they may produce vast numbers of irrelevant results. They work best when you have a fairly specific topic and when you use search techniques such as Boolean operators and phrase searching with quotation marks.

AltaVista <www.altavista.com>
Allows basic and advanced searching of Websites, images, audio, and video media.

Google <www.google.com>
Allows basic and advanced, and image searching of Web sites, as well as limited search directory features with History listed under "Society."

HotBot <www.hotbot.lycos.com>
Allows simple and advanced searching, of Web sites, images, audio, and visual media, as well as limited search directory features with History listed under "Society."

SEARCH DIRECTORIES

Search directories list Web sites organized by subject, with the "site editors" providing some level of evaluation. A good directory may lead you to information more quickly than a search engine, especially if your topic is fairly broad, as directories return a more selective, set of results. History subjects are not consistently indexed; they can be listed under such headings as "Humanities" and "Social Science."

Librarian's Index to the Internet <lii.org>
Indexes History under "Arts, Crafts, & Humanities."

Open Directory Project <dmoz.com>
Indexes History under "Society."

WWW Virtual Library <www.vlib.org>
Indexes History under "Humanities."

METASEARCH ENGINES

Metasearch engines search multiple search engines simultaneously but they do not return detailed results.

Ixquick <www.ixquick.com>
Searches eleven search engines and also allows MP3, pictures, and news searching.

MetaCrawler <www.metacrawler.com>
Searches eleven search engines.

Vivisimo <vivisimo.com>
Searches four search engines, plus news, business, government, and other search services.

GENERAL HISTORY INTERNET SITES

Academic Info History Gateway <www.academicinfo.com/hist.html>
Provides links to world history, country, regional, and topical resources.

Digital Librarian <www.digital-librarian.com/history.html>
Links to regional and topical resources.

Fordham University Internet History Sourcebook Project <www.fordham.edu/halsall/>
Includes links to primary regional and topical sourcebooks.

Hiram College Library World Wide Web Resources in History <library.hiram.edu/sub_history.htm>
Organized by gateways, geographical regions, special topics, and multimedia resources.

Internet Public Library History <www.ipl.org/div/subject/browse/hum30.00.00/>
Provides links by region, era, topic, documents, and sources.

Princeton University Library History Resources <www.princeton.edu/~pressman/history.htm>
Organized by gateways, full-text sources, time periods, regions and countries, and selected topics.

University of Idaho Repositories of Primary Sources <www.uidaho.edu/special-collections/Other.Repositories.html>
Lists worldwide sites for primary source manuscripts, archives, books, and photographs.

Virginia Tech University Libraries Selected Free Web Resources for History <www.lib.vt.edu/subjects/hist/hist-net.html>
Organized by gateways, eras, and regions.

WWW Virtual Library's History Central Catalogue <www.ukans.edu/history/VL>
Alphabetical list by general topic, including general research methods and materials, eras and epochs, historical topics, and geographical regions.

SPECIALIZED SITES FOR HISTORICAL RESEARCH

North America

American Memory: Historical Collections for the National Digital Library <memory.loc.gov/ammem/amhome.html>
Presents over 100 multimedia collections of digitized documents, photographs, recorded sound, moving pictures, and text.

America's Story from America's Library <www.americaslibrary.gov/cgi-bin/page.cgi>
Presents links to primary source documents exploring American history through its people, places, and events.

Archiving Early America <earlyamerica.com/>

Focuses on primary source material from eighteenth-century America, including original newspapers, maps, and writings.

The Gilder Lehrman Institute of American History Collection <www.gliah.uh.edu/index.cfm>

One of the largest private collections of documents in American history. It includes print materials, maps, photographs, quizzes, glossaries, and links to other sites.

National Park Service — Links to the Past <www.cr.nps.gov/>

Explores America's historical and cultural past with links to people, places, objects, and events.

Presidential Libraries <www.archives.gov/presidential_libraries/addresses/addresses.html>

Links to the presidential libraries from the U.S. National Archives and Records Administration.

United States Civil War Center <www.cwc.lsu.edu/>

Promotes the study of the Civil War from various perspectives.

Worldwide

Ancient Egypt <www.ancientegypt.co.uk/menu.html>

Explores Egyptian life, the pyramids, and mummification.

EuroDocs: Primary Historical Documents from Western Europe <library.byu.edu/~rdh/eurodocs>

Provides links to key documents, organized by country and period.

Exploring Ancient World Cultures <eawc.evansville.edu/index.htm>

Features essays and primary texts on Near East, India, Egypt, China, Greece, Rome, Early Islam, and Medieval Europe. Includes chronologies, images, texts, and Web links.

Historical Text Archive <www.historicaltextarchive.com>

Collection of historical documents in electronic format from several countries, and in several topical areas.

The History Channel <www.historychannel.com>

Search by topic, keyword, or century. Includes speeches, discussion groups, study guides, and online museum exhibits.

The History Net: Where History Lives on the Web <www.thehistorynet.com>

Search by topic or publication for links to numerous sites, including select electronic journals.

The History of the Crusades <libtext.library.wisc.edu/HistCrusades>

The online edition of a six-volume narrative history. Both the individual volumes and the series can be browsed and searched by keyword.

The History Place: The Past into the Future <www.historyplace.com>

Offers links to documents, photos, and timelines.

The Labyrinth <labyrinth.georgetown.edu/>

Provides access to electronic resources in medieval studies. Search by category, type of materials, or keyword.

Medieval Academy of America <www.medievalacademy.org/>
Offers online articles from the *Medieval Academy News*, as well as links to other Web sites.

NetSERF: The Internet Connection to Medieval Resources <www.netserf.org/>
Links to sites on various aspects of medieval life, including history, arts, culture, literature, music, religion, and women.

Online Reference Book for Medieval Studies <http://orb.rhodes.edu>
Written and maintained by medieval scholars, this site offers an encyclopedia, online texts, and links to other online resources.

Portals to the World <www.loc.gov/rr/international/portals.html>
This site provides links to electronic resources from around the world, with country information on history, politics, culture, business, and travel.

Royal Historical Society Bibliography <www.rhs.ac.uk/bibwel.html>
This online edition of the Society's *Annual Bibliographies* includes items not published in the print or CD-ROM editions.

Rulers <rulers.org/>
Lists heads of state and government of all countries and territories, along with a list of religious leaders. Offers links to online sources for political leaders and elections around the world. Monthly updates are posted.

INTERNET SITES OF SPECIAL INTEREST

The following Web sites can connect you to electronic discussion groups and with electronic library catalogs.

Humanities and Social Science Online <www2.h-net.msu.edu>
A consortium of scholars and teachers that sponsors electronic newsletters to encourage communication about current research and teaching.

LibDex <www.libdex.com/>
A worldwide directory of online library catalogs. Browse the index by country or by library name.

Library of Congress <lcweb.loc.gov>
Searching the catalogs and collections including the American Memory Project, an Online Gallery of Exhibitions (with text and illustrations), and a legislative information search directory (THOMAS).

ELECTRONIC JOURNALS AND MAGAZINES

An increasing number of periodicals are available in electronic format through the Internet. Some contain entire issues while others limit access to selective articles. Your library may subscribe to electronic journals and online periodical databases, making them available with appropriate password authentication. The following Web sites can help you locate electronic periodicals by title and topic.

Internet Public Library Newspapers <www.ipl.org/div/news/>
Lists online newspapers from around the world.

Internet Public Library Serials <www.ipl.org/div/serials/>
Lists online periodicals from around the world.

WWW-Virtual Library <www.history-journals.de/>
The History Journals Guide.

Index

Directory to Documentation Models